CONTEXTS

Vol. 2

MEDIUMS

Pratt Sessions

Contexts

David Erdman
New Architectural Contexts

One half of the Pratt Sessions focuses on New Architectural Contexts. The intention of focusing on this subject is to sharpen "context" within our own terms as a set of graduate programs on the East Coast. We see context as a vague, sloppy, and ill-defined term that continues to be propped up as the holy grail of architectural authenticity, communal value, and appropriateness, and yet is limited in its usage; theoretical and/or practical examinations. For us, context nicely encapsulates an array of contemporary debates ranging from the socio-political inequities of development to environmental responsiveness and is here, through the Pratt Sessions, placed on the chopping block as a means to principally investigate whether or not these two aspects of contexts *are* really the kingpins of 21st-century urban, suburban, and rural contexts or simply just decoys and marketing terms used to prop up otherwise mediocre buildings and site strategies.

The aim of these three sessions is to examine the eccentricities of the 21st century-city at-large—its density, its fragility, its inequity, its experiential qualities, and its design opportunities—through the lens of various established and emerging designers' and thinkers' working in New York City and Los Angeles through the lens of disciplinary thinkers who identify our anxiety and ecstasy of influence and through the lens of philosophical discourse on realism. This triad of sessions and focuses are an intentional shift from understanding the city as a language, a pattern, and quantitative data toward an understanding that is indiscernibly about urbanity and its "live," real, muted, and yet unknown qualities. Each of the Pratt Sessions participants offers a vantage point on the subject of contexts: architectural, theoretical, and philosophical. Each pairing raises specific questions surrounding the prospect of those subjects: namely what is context, how might it pertain to architecture and, why would our renewed understanding of it be valuable now or in the future?

From invigorated understandings of housing's material and circulatory dimensions, to examinations of how we sample and borrow influences both adjacent to sites and from the discipline, to ways in which philosophical objects and processes underpin the perceived and evasive qualities of cities, the designers and thinkers comprising these three Pratt Sessions suggest a turn in our understanding of context. Each participant is accomplished if not lauded for their range of projects and approach to the design of context, for their rigorous research on the representational methods of context or as scholars who have wholly reconceived context through philosophical frameworks.

The sessions skirt and directly affront a disciplinary etymology of the word "context," which is complex and multifaceted. This meandering and range of approach from the oblique to the head on is intentional. We use the term context to frame this lobe of the Pratt Sessions series to perturb and agitate our participants, their work, and our attendant audiences into a conversation about what is otherwise a sensitive subject. To set up the discussion we have accounted for what we understand to be two mainstream disciplinary benchmarks that are common hallmarks of undergraduate and graduate curricula (Pratt's included).

The first benchmark is one that situates context in its semiological capacities. The diligent "contextualist" in this scenario is one whose project appears like and has a logical slash meaningful relationship with its adjacent surroundings. At best, context in this instantiation signifies the past and its origins while having the potential to inflect or distort both in some manner. Techniques of collage or encapsulating specific geographic typologies in the form of regionalist vernaculars and/or borrowing adjacent materialities anchor this benchmark. Think Colin Rowe, Aldo Rossi, and Kenneth Frampton. Or in a more contemporary context, consider Shigeru Ban, Wang Shu, and Peter Zumthor. These are all architects whose discourse is perhaps the closest thing we have to a "slow food" movement in architecture. It embodies work that has a strong communal innuendo if nothing else. Their work represents the "new authentic."

The second arm, and an outcome of the digital turn in the late 20th century, is one that sees context as environment of data and processes; often misconstrued as an "ecology," which can be mapped. The metrics of solar orientation, rising tides, diminishing cooling loads, socio-economic and political data are among other quantitative factors that may drive the design;

data stands in as an alibi legitimating a form-finding logic. This results in a design-by-inevitability logic. "I'm a designer, I want to harness the context, I map all the forces, and that results in a building." Think parametric in whatever form it may rear its head.

On behalf of our students, their curiosity, and their future, we are not okay with this being the terminal reservoir of context: with these two approaches/methods being the limit of ideas for a definitive architectural (or broader understanding of) context. How do we account for buildings that do not appear anything like their surroundings and, while being environmentally responsible, do not necessarily flaunt those parameters as their formal alibi? Perhaps even more important is the subject of origin, authenticity, and ontology. Does the site always come first and the architecture second?

New Architectural Contexts is thus an area of research in the GAUD and the Pratt Sessions that explores the ways in which architecture activates context; something we understand as an explicit symptom of 21st-century cities as they become increasingly more dense and as they grow inward and accumulate on top of themselves to conserve resources—cultural, economic, and ecological. Shifting the discourse on "architecture and the city" away from the semiological and away from quantitative performance-based design, the focus in the sessions is understanding architectural context as that which is fundamentally premised on the design of urban qualities.

The reformulation of architectural praxes that results from this re-centering of context in the discipline is of equal interest and a center point of each of the architectural practices encapsulated in these conversations and sessions, as well as the extradisciplinary implications of writing/theorizing and our corollary and complimentary understanding of context that overlap with and parallel, similarly evolving principles in philosophy. The flattening of ontologies, lack of anxiety about influence, and ingenious ways in which existing buildings or materialities are recycled produce a constellation of potential ways in which to newly understand an over-used/misused term in architecture. Disciplinary and temporal boundaries, inequities and ontologies in these discussions are placed on common ground opening up a variety of ways in which context can be provocative and imbue architects with agency in the complex decision-making chains of the built environment.

"New" is thus not intended as a descriptor for the unfounded or exotic geographies yet to be colonized by progressive design and/or technology nor a search for an essentialistic regionally-based authentic. It is not necessarily even concerned with what is next. "New" is instead what is right in front of our eyes. In the framework of these sessions it is a blunt admission that the cities we operate in and the things (objects) we make no longer fit the morphological patterns of the prior century, nor that our resultant disciplinary apparatus is well-formed for engaging the contemporary or future city. New thinking, new understanding, new approaches that alter and allow us to recapitulate existing cites, existing villages and, existing sites is the new we are seeking; with a fresh eye toward the multitude of praxes and disciplines we can engage. This is the focus of these sessions and what we believe to be a pertinent discussion to the future city and profession.

Michael Maltzan

Gregg Pasquarelli

01

02

03

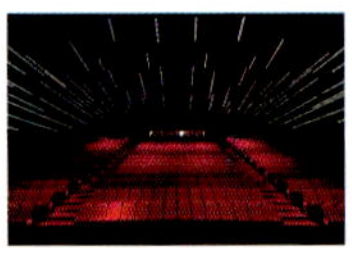

04

05

06

07

08

09

10

11

12

16

17

13

14

15

18

Introduction

DAVID ERDMAN

It's my pleasure to welcome Michael Maltzan and Gregg Pasquarelli this evening. Both of these architects and their practices are thriving, each engaging a multitude of project types, scales, and clients.

While both firms work nationally and internationally, it is important to recognize that they are equally emblematic of the cities in which they are based, and share some related methodologies: specifically the deep interest in making that is physically enmeshed into their respective office cultures and evident in the modalities through which they investigate their ideas—principally via models.

I am hoping tonight we can discuss how their work (particularly in the realm of housing) opens up contemporary and useful ways we might define architectural context and its related understandings of density—be it population density, building density, or otherwise.

Michael's work contains a trace and subtle use of graphics, font, and color. 01 These devices may give definition to or up-end some of his massing and organizational strategies. They intervene at a number of different scales. 02 03 What he often refers to is the elastic qualities one might interpret as the interaction and dynamics found between the geometry of mass, between organizations, and between graphic types. Operations like slicing or bending give his projects a subtle set of experiential effects. 04

One might identify circulation as a second area of interest in Michael's work; it is meticulously managed and woven into the fabric of form and mass. 05 "Circuitry" is rendered in section, three-dimensionally, embedded, or exposed. 06 It is imbued with an operative agency. Circuits span the variegated milieus of a building or a structure (public/private, indoor/outdoor, above/below) through pulses of thickness and immersion. 07

The body of residential work, specifically affordable housing, located in downtown Los Angeles, sets both a turning point and benchmark for affordable housing at large and the work of MMA. The projects are dense and compact. They deploy color in atypical ways. 08 One could cite historic examples where color used to break down large, singular massing blocks, diminishing their scale; or cite other instances where color might be utilized to augment architectural articulation and depth; all techniques borrowed from largely 2D practices like painting or graphic design. There is anxiety in the discipline and profession, which has discursively understood these techniques as "superficial," "illusive," "trickery" deployed when there is literally no space or depth to build them. In other words, one might understand them as "fake" architectural techniques.

Michael's uses of color, graphic texture, and pattern is, one could argue, significantly more explicitly beholden to architectural discourse and thinking. As an example, you get chromatic hints of virtually implied interiors. Color can enhance circulatory direction or "reflect" across corners. There's a dialogue and tension between interior and exterior masses and color that intensifies cracks between the massing; where often, in his work, color is tucked in and "secreted" away. Those cracks and their veiled appearances on the exterior eventually give way to spaces where color is intensely saturated. This is using color in a haptic way that elongates duration of experience while producing and enriching spatial relationships and tensions between different contexts and zones.

Carver Housing is an excellent example. Through a black and gray, texturally stepped circuit, delivering one from the perimeter to the central courtyard, the occupant is transported into a kaleidoscopic, lush void-space saturates with color and shadow play. 09 It is through this example that one can identify in Michael's recent work an effort to move away from physics of typical affordable housing, tower in the park, or the proverbial decorated chunky, dense masses and their use of illusive trickery in the past. The experience of these housing projects is surprising, lulls you inward, and builds communal spaces of interiority that are vibrant and dynamic; they intertwine color, circuitry, texture, and mass to build a contemporary, empowered social-politic affordability that moves into new concepts of the superficial.

If Michael's work is "painterly and graphic," I would posit Gregg's work with SHoP is deeply material. From their early exhibitions, which are an incredible way of seeing the potential for future larger scale work, SHoP has focused on materially based tectonic experiments. 10 11 Texture, patterning, and linework often evolve from those installations into strategies for larger projects. 12 13

There is a specific material sensibility bound to their projects. Extensive measures are put into place to render sheen as matte and to bring to the foreground the temporal, patinated dimensions of materials. There is a willingness to embrace decay and entropy, where rusting COR-TEN steel or slowly degrading wood builds characteristics and gives their projects a registration of time and depth. [14] One could say that, similar to Michael, here too we find an interest in the surface and its resonant capacities, though perhaps a chemical and molecular focus more than one that draws upon traditions of illusion; let's call it a working theory of bas relief. [15]

Because of these concepts of materiality and the way they're working with 2 and 2.5 dimensions, their housing projects may look familiar, but they don't emulate immediately consumable relationships to their surroundings. The highly repetitious and dominating "mainframe" of housing is materially and, by result, contextually hacked. The use of zinc, black brick, and textural patterning suggests an alternative way of working with materials that is less about reinforcing its surroundings than transforming and galvanizing them. [16] [17]

In their recent American Copper towers in Manhattan, for example, materials that would be commonly used as a highlight or a roofing material are instead used across the entirety of the two towers. The staggered matrix pattern of brown-gold copper facade panels will transform into a teal-green patina over time. The temporal aspect of the materiality starts to operate at a radical scale, cascading what is historically and urbanistically aerial—accented roofs—down to the ground and onto the river; animating and energizing this newly founded mid-town epicenter within Kips Bay. [18] This approach to material is something they continue to explore in their tallest, most "compact" projects—two supertowers, one in Manhattan and one in Brooklyn.

So how *do* these firms engage architectural context? Are they mimicking it through the specificities of their geographies along the lines of a semiological discourse we can all recognize? Certainly comparisons of "contextual approach" could be drawn: some aspects of the work being more abstractly driven, others more historically driven. Are they responding environmentally; justifying their forms through quantitative, parametric, urban, and/or environmental analysis?

Or, are they in the same state of confusion the discipline faces—a sort of diluted and mixed bag of ideas, none of which have an exactitude nor forge a clear path articulating how design engages context?

I would like to suggest how Gregg, Michael, and their respective firms are in fact driving projects and responding to issues that are not quite evident yet in the context "as is"; specifically that they are designing for a density and context yet to arrive.

All indicators suggest that cities need to densify and absorb housing in the coming 25 to 50 years. We are feeling the effects in New York City via super towers that exhibit immense building density as well as the raw population density increases we are seeing nearby in downtown Brooklyn. In LA and surrounding neighborhoods there are plans to intensify and densify Wilshire Boulevard, the first projects of which are rearing their heads.

While many architects focus on recycled materials or power supply, there is a tendency to overlook the fact that density is the front line of the environmental problem. When you look across the globe, cities like Hong Kong stand out. Their extremely concentrated density affords them significant benefits; among them low levels of consumption. Why? Because of density, you are moving things shorter distances and people walk a lot, resulting in significant efficiencies.

Residential buildings and commercial are "small game" compared to transport when looking at global issues forecast by various international organizations. The issue is how do we, as architects productively and creatively engage that density, which reduces transit.

Michael and Gregg are working on the frontlines of density. What I find significant is that they are focused on how to understand the current and future contexts of their projects qualitatively. They embrace density and find its qualities; their work has an implicit and explicit interiority. This is an interiority that requires them to "dig-in" and find spaces of opportunity and palpable qualities within the confines of highly constrained, super-dense, super-tall buildings as well as to unleash the potentials to re-read, to understand, and to theorize typologies and histories within the discipline.

Michael Maltzan

LOS ANGELES, CA

Like many architects of my generation, I was raised in an architecture that saw housing as one of the fundamental typologies of modernism. It was a project type where architects strove to intertwine housing with the most progressive and optimistic approaches toward space, technology, and ideas about living in politics. Through that work, I came to believe that architecture was a real agent of change and progress.

Projects like the Weissenhofsiedlung (1927) are a part of our collective history as architects. We know images of the project, generally very optimistic, as a concept of the new and progressive world. We also know images, which are as much burned into a larger collective social framework, that have become icons of architecture's perceived role in the diminishment of the progressive possibilities of housing and largely divorced from the complexities of the surrounding city. Out of this deeply complicated history of modernism, architecture lost its role as an agent of ideas and solutions.

The emergence of the single-family house in postwar American suburbs largely overrode the conversation about collective and multi-family housing in cities, as well as many of the defining issues of the city itself—identity, density, and community, to name just a few. In a city like Los Angeles, the expectations of what the single-family house produces or can offer are a romantic hangover of what the single-family house is. It still characterizes how we talk about the expectations of our living spaces.

In many cities, especially in LA, the manifest destiny-like sprawl to the periphery has slowed. Density, mobility, affordability, and community are pressing concerns. Housing is, again, an important model for understanding how we address these priorities, but also, and maybe most importantly, for how we begin to imagine the city. Architecture's role, especially housing, and how to anticipate the future city are driving forces in the work that I'm going to present.

I deeply believe that housing is nothing less than a microcosm of the city itself, whether it's the individual unit, the individual house, or the multi-family house. Experimenting with the single-family residence plays very heavily into the way that we think about multi-family housing. I want to start with a house that is fundamental to the housing type in California and still very much a part of people's expectation.

This is the Pittman Dowell Residence, which is in La Crescenta, right at the edge of the sprawl of the San Gabriel Valley and the San Gabriel Mountains. There is an existing house, built by Richard Neutra in the 1950s for his assistant and assistant's husband. Because Neutra had an almost socialist

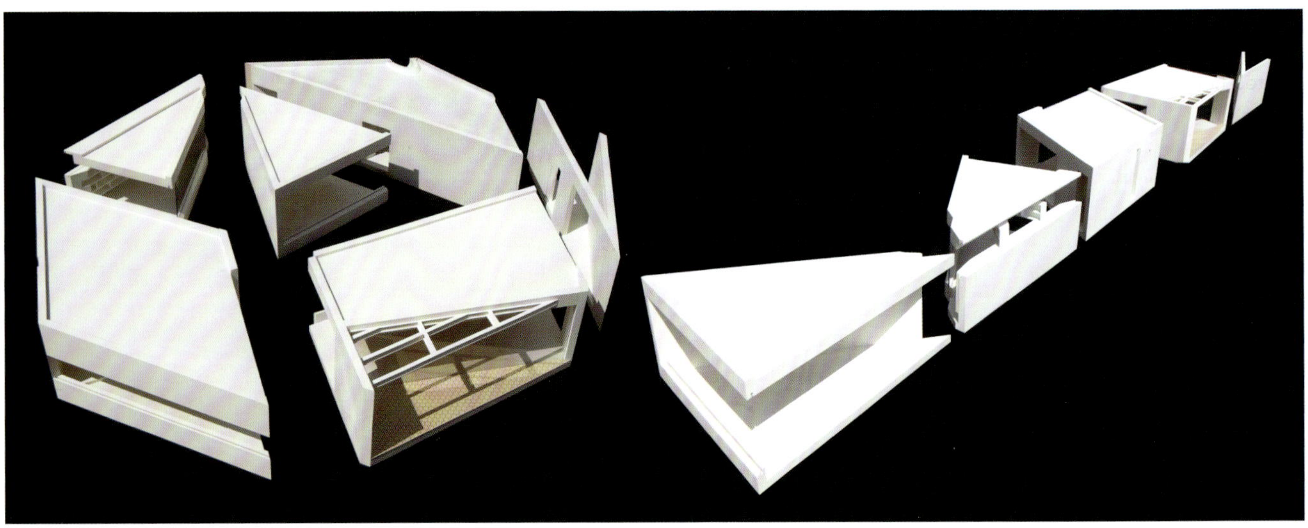

Michael Maltzan Architecture, Pittman Dowell Residence, La Crescenta, CA, 2009

Michael Maltzan Architecture, Pittman Dowell Residence, La Crescenta, CA, 2009

ambition toward housing, he built this property to have three other pads. His idea was that this wouldn't be the only house and that eventually a small progressive community might be created here.

The house that we designed occupies one of the pads that was never developed. You spiral up to the house from the valley, always with views out to that typical suburban context. You eventually arrive at a courtyard with a carport, as opposed to a garage, detached from the house. The house is very inward-looking in contrast to the Neutra house, which is a quintessential postwar modernist house—designed by a notable architect and a type of architecture that found form stylistically in many of the tract houses that were built in Los Angeles, Southern California, and across the United States. The postwar modernist house was marked by a series of ideas, like incredible transparency between inside and out, a great lightness, and a thin structural frame.

Our Pittman Dowell Residence was meant to be the alter ego of the Neutra house. It adopts Neutra's transparency of the exterior and instead makes it the inside of the house, while the exterior is about the solidity and opaqueness that you might find at the center of the Neutra house with its traditional fireplace.

Our clients felt that in our contemporary world, where we are connected all the time through our devices, they wanted to rebel against that sense of constant transparency. Instead, they looked for a house that would have a greater deal of interiority. In plan, the house has a clockwise movement around the central courtyard, but you can also short-circuit across the courtyards, because all the glass starts to slide open. With the exception of some closets, the guest bathroom, and the front door, the house has no doors in it. It's meant to be a house that sits between a modern idea of the open plan and one that still has a conventional series of rooms. On the inside, there is a great sense of transparency through individual spaces, so that the bathroom, the bedroom, the courtyard, and the living room are all connected to each other in visible ways.

We have been working in the downtown area of Los

Angeles for several years on affordable housing, specifically for individuals who were formerly homeless. We have been working with a group called the Skid Row Housing Trust to build affordable and quite dense community housing. Star Apartments, which has 101 units, is our third project with the Trust. Each one has evolved slightly from the last based on slight changes in demographics, but they all built off the same template. They're projects that are meant to bring together a group of individuals who have generally not lived in a community. The goal is not just to produce a house, but to jumpstart a small urban community in these buildings.

One of the things that characterizes the Star Apartments project was the goal of reusing an existing building as a part of the new building. The Trust is very committed to developing lively partnerships with the city by bringing in more mixed-use in the buildings. This is unusual in LA because of the way that the money comes to these projects. If you're taking housing money to build these projects, you can't do things like retail, but the Trust found a loophole. If you have an existing building that has existing retail, you can keep that retail space. They bought this building for us to work with.

The existing building has a concrete roof with parking on top. In most cases in LA, you would've scraped this building clean, but we kept it. We created a podium on top and built the apartments above what is now the new social and community deck.

We were very interested in hyper density for this project. Again, going back to the single-family house with a garden around it, here we are trying to create as thick a series of units as possible with the idea that horizontal space would start to become the equivalent of that collective yard. A horizontal space in the middle is a social space with a number of passive and active programs. There's a jogging track around the entire space, a series of classrooms, and a community kitchen, a half-court basketball court that's now turned into a pickleball court, and community gardens. These are all meant to create opportunities for the residents to develop a neighborhood in the building.

The last project I want to talk about is One Santa Fe. The LA River runs along the site to East Boyle Heights, which is very much the power center of Latino culture in the city. There are train tracks and high-power lines that run along both sides of the river. It's a corridor of intense infrastructure. This building was beginning to think about scale and density, using the form of infrastructure as a way of thinking about what that looks like in a city like Los Angeles, as opposed to more traditional models

Michael Maltzan Architecture, Star Apartments, Los Angeles, CA, 2014

Michael Maltzan Architecture, One Santa Fe, Los Angeles, CA, 2015

of density.

The building, on the one hand, is an incredibly visible building from certain parts of the city. At other times, given its horizontality, the texture of its facades, the different scale treatments, it intentionally fades into the middle ground of the city. The ground level is primarily all retail. There are two bridges in the building that create a pass-through to a gold or red line transit station, which does not yet exist, but will be built here in the next few years.

Parking was a challenge. Even though we could negotiate lower parking for the project, because of its connection to some of these emerging transit systems, we still had to have quite a bit of parking under the wider section of the site. Where the building gets very thin, because it is literally between an MTA maintenance building and the street, we couldn't go below grade with the parking, so the parking gets raised up to the second and third floor with the anticipation that, eventually, as cars become fewer and fewer, they can turn into loft spaces.

The building uses some of the existing context intentionally, trying to allude to the idea that, almost like a palimpsest, one way of building density in this city can be to build up vertically. As you move down the length of the building, you find moments that are generally very pragmatic, like the circulation up to the parking. There is a contingent set of moves all along the building, which starts to lock it into the context around it. There's a wide range of units in this building. It's one of the ways that we're trying to deal with affordability—not by designating a certain chunk of the building as an affordable section, but creating everything from four-bedroom, eight-person units to very small micro-units, which produces an expansive set of economic points in the project.

I want to finish by just talking about this idea of scale. I think scale relates to density, although they have different ambitions, attitudes, and histories. We've been criticized in this building that it was too big for the context; that it's a behemoth, spaceship, or ocean liner. I think that criticism is exactly right if you believe that a city like Los Angeles and its context is going to remain as it is today over the next few decades. However, in cities that are changing, it's the responsibility of architects and planners to think about buildings as forecast, a development that tries to meet the city and its future; to speculate about what that density might look like in the next generation.

Michael Maltzan Architecture, New Carver Apartments, Los Angeles, CA, 2015

Gregg Pasquarelli

NEW YORK, NY

SHoP came together for one reason: we wanted to challenge the notion of paper versus executive architects. Architecture is an open framework; it is about being both a thinker and a maker. We weren't afraid of the technical and political issues, and the financial systems that help drive architecture.

We do a lot of work around the world but we are really a New York firm. From the very beginning, we were thinking about public space, densification, and how to use the underused places in New York. Every square inch of this island is fought over constantly. One of our very early projects was the East River Waterfront, which was then an area of abandoned docks and an elevated highway system. The idea was to densify this stretch of the waterfront by building up ground planes in order to create parks where they didn't exist.

That project led us to work the South Street Seaport, which was an interior-oriented shopping mall on the waterfront. It was meant to attract tourists while hiding the fabric of this undesirable neighborhood. We again focused on densifying this area, connecting it to the grid across and under the highway, and to make a new "urban village" on the water. We've always been interested in the waterfront and we've worked on multiple projects that recapture such areas of New York City.

To shift this presentation to housing, as was suggested, I want to present three projects. The first one is the American Copper Buildings, a project on the east side of Manhattan. We always draw from context, thinking about what the neighborhood is and how it works. The effects of a building always radiate out and we're equally interested in how the city radiates in. Here, we were working with a poorly executed master plan, which put a public school on the southwest corner and a park on the northeast corner, allowing for two towers in between. The park would always be in shade, underneath the highway and facing east.

We felt like we needed to make a context where there almost wasn't one. We wanted to make a neighborhood for the residents. So rather than creating two amenity spaces—one in each building—the idea was to create one great space for everyone.

We wanted to skin the north and south facades in a material. We tend to use materials that don't have applied finishes to them, so they will age and patina naturally. The idea was to radiate a pattern from the moment where the bridge connects the two buildings to create a moiré effect. We decided to use raw copper so that it would arrive like a shiny penny but at some point, it will turn green like the Statue of Liberty. It is almost a performance art piece for the city.

American Copper was a project we had to do with brutal zoning and no context, but the next two projects have a stronger context. 9 DeKalb in Downtown Brooklyn is located on a triangular site with a phenomenal landmark building—an old Dime Savings Bank that is both an exterior and an interior landmark.

The original architects dealt with this triangular site by using six-sided stars or hexagons to resolve the geometry. We took those triangular lines and laid them across the site, and then we started to think about a series of interlocking hexagons for the tower. When you're in Manhattan, you always have a primary avenue crossing a secondary street. From a design perspective, you always know the way someone will view the building. But in Brooklyn the different street grids don't align, and especially as this is going to be the tallest building in Brooklyn, we didn't want any side to have a primary or secondary face. The idea was to spiral the setbacks of the hexagons as they go up. We were looking at contemporary versions of crenelation.

We have a color palette that goes from white to bronze

SHoP Architects, East River Waterfront, New York, NY, 2011

SHoP Architects, Pier 15, New York, NY, 2018

to black. We started to abstract many forms out of the bank and made 1,500 to 2,000 different shapes and sizes in the colors. Then, we started making pattern books of how the facade would look. To get a depth and a mixture of color, pilasters come out up to 18 inches of the facade in hundreds of different sizes and six different materials.

We had to get approval from the Landmark Preservation Commission to build this up through the old bank building. Its phenomenal interior will become part of the lobby and retail space but is currently in terrible condition. To connect the bank to the tower, we designed what we call the "convexacave column," which we will mill out of solid marble and will then become the columns that wrap around the new part of the building.

The last project I want to show is 111 West 57th Street. In looking at the buildings that New Yorkers love, like the Empire State Building and Chrysler Building, many people will say, "It's because they are historic." But we think that people love them because of their proportion. These early 20th-century buildings created a skyline that was focused on light getting into the street. In addition, issues like getting light into buildings and no air conditioning made for tall slender buildings. Of course, post-World War II, with the invention of air conditioning and with American efficiency, you start to see the emergence of 30,000-foot floor plates in projects like the Pan Am building. They give you a different skyline. Right now, we're in a moment where there are so few air rights left that whatever can be grabbed will be pushed up to get a view of the park. In addition, the technology for the structure allows us to deal with the acceleration of super tall and slender towers. These create a third skyline typology.

Our building, 111 West 57th Street, had to go on top of and next to a landmark, Steinway Hall. Our client bought a vacant lot and Steinway Hall and we could've built a building just on the vacant lot, adding all the air rights from a good portion of the rest of the block. But this would've blocked much of Steinway Hall. We made an argument to the city, "Let us build on top of the landmark. We'll slide it back and open it up and let light into this area to celebrate that building, but maybe you let us put 1,400 ft. on top of it and you won't notice."

We started to play with the notion of a setback, thinking about context and the historical way it was done. The contemporary way to set back is just to express the sky exposure plane, but our idea was for a feathered setback.

We opened up the north and south facade with glass to offer views of the park. We had a very thick shear wall on the sides. To avoid this looking like an ominous building, we started thinking about performative ornament. We knew that texture would create turbulence and slow down movement of the building. The facade is made up of a series of CNC-fabricated terracotta pilasters, which each become a setback and together create a pattern. Between the terracotta, we added a cast bronze filigree, like sinewy tissue.

We were able to get approvals for the building in four months, which saved the client tens of millions of dollars in interest payments. He put this money right back into the building and we did not have one single element value-engineered in the whole project. We argued, "The building is only 60 units, but eight million New Yorkers have to look at it every day so you better spend at least as much on the outside as you do on the inside." The client said, "Absolutely. You're right," and never questioned anything that we wanted to do on the facade.

Thinking about technology and sustainability is terrific. These are great things but there are two things we can really

SHoP Architects, Pier 17, New York, NY, 2018

do as architects. One thing is to build density. Build it near mass transit, where you're going to get the biggest bang for the buck. When we build these buildings, we have to design great public space around them because if we're going to live in super dense cities, we need that public space. The other thing that architects can do is to build buildings that people love, so they're not renovating every 20 years.

Architects have a place at the table right now and if there's an engagement in the political process, the financial process, the technological issues, the design issues, the public space, the density, and the connection to mass transit, we have a chance to make a huge impact on the way cities continue to get built and their impact on the earth.

SHoP Architects, American Copper Buildings, New York, NY, 2018

SHoP Architects, 9 DeKalb, Brooklyn, NY, Under Construction

SHoP Architects, 111 West 57th Street, New York, NY, Under Construction

SHoP Architects, Pier 17, New York, NY, 2018

Conversation

MICHAEL MALTZAN AND GREGG PASQUARELLI

David Erdman: While anthropologically in North America, there is anxiety about living in density, if you look at the general history of humanity, there's no reason we'd be living in New York City if we didn't have a desire to be closely surrounded by other people. Both of your housing projects are very dense. It's great to have you together in this conversation because we can look at this sense of density in different ways.

I find these projects to be innovative models in terms of how North Americans look at domesticity. These projects figure out creative ways to develop productive qualities of interiority or objecthood that aren't problematic. Is that something you are talking about in your offices?

Michael Maltzan: I think that anxiety toward density is absolutely correct. There's a real psychological and emotional response to it. In a city like Los Angeles, which has staked a great deal of its identity on the alternative to density, it has been more challenging to have those conversations. But I think it's shifting. It is perhaps a generational change, where the younger generation is increasingly looking to areas like the Arts District, which is exploding, as an alternative way to live in the city.

Some of that has to do with changes in lifestyle, such as the way we work today, since we don't all work in a centralized place anymore. A lot of it also has to do with the change in the perception of the car as a primary component of our sense of freedom. For the younger generation, those under 30 years old, it doesn't have that same attraction.

All of this is putting pressure on evolving the concept of density in the city. It doesn't change the need for a lot of other social spaces and mechanisms, which Gregg started to touch on at the end of his presentation, to supplement ways of living.

Erdman: Hong Kong is the only city currently performing at consumption levels that the Paris Accord wants to see in global cities by 2026. This is because of Hong Kong's density, which lives on only one third of its footprint. It has an urban amenity and you need those other counterpart spaces to go with it.

Gregg Pasquarelli: It doesn't work if you don't have that moment to breathe. In a single-family house, five sides of your six-sided cube are exposed to the elements and therefore, you're wasting energy. If you live in a high-rise apartment, five sides of your dwelling unit are sharing heating and cooling with your neighbor. It's a fundamental difference in the way you have to think about what it means to live on this planet, what it means to share resources, and what it means to be responsible. After World War II, a very political and strategic series of elements forced New York to get gutted out by itself and force people to go out to the suburbs; whether it was redlining or civil defense, it was about making a decent quality of life. Once they created some decent schools and parks again, everyone came right back to the city. It took greater effort to destroy the city than it did to bring it back.

Erdman: There's no way to argue that any of your projects look like anything around then. But one way into that is this sense of interiority. In many ways, it's the only choice in New York because you've got to activate your projects perfectly.

Pasquarelli: Each unit is getting smaller and smaller but we've created communal spaces. In New York, it was a generation of those under 50 years old that didn't want to live in the suburbs or have a car. But today, it's only those under 30 who actually use the communal spaces in the building. These spaces are becoming increasingly important. We try to work at three scales with this: the communal space that those in the community use, the communal space that is shared with the city, and then thinking about the building as a kind of amenity that's shared with the entire city.

Erdman: As the 21st century densifies, it's going to fold back on itself. Not only will we have to build more housing, but we'll probably have to build on top of preexisting structures. Both of you have tested aggressive models of alteration. Gregg, you did this in two of the project you presented here, and Michael, you dealt less with a landmark directly, but you presented a strong strategy with your Pittman Dowell Residence.

Maltzan: Whenever you're trying to preserve something, there always has to be an argument for why you would do that. For me, it's often a question of sustainability; if you're going to tear down preexisting structures every time, there's an enormous amount of materials that you are losing. I do think that there's an approach to making in the city to produce density, which is going to push us to start reusing more. How you start that conversation is something that's not on a lot of people's radar. But architects have the ability to bring up that argument and show what the benefits are on so many levels.

Erdman: Most architecture schools still teach only how to design a building from the ground up. Historic preservation has never been seen as career-building work. While there are many projects by well-known architects that dealt with reuse, they are generally not lauded in that light.

Now, there are other cultural and political arguments that one can begin to associate with bigger issues of city building and how that could actually become a strategy to find projects or a way into the city.

Pasquarelli: Yes, we're not teaching students the idea that sometimes you've got to make your own projects, invent your own things, or find the solution. Sometimes you have to look for the anomaly in the market so you can have a positive benefit on the city as a whole, as a way toward Architecture with a capital A. Taking equity positions or partnering with the owner can sometimes allow you a chance to innovate in way that you never would have if you're just the hired gun.

This definition of contextuality as something that looks like everything next to it is ridiculous. For us, the Porter House (2003) was the first time we worked on a project as a joint venture; we found it, we put the deal together, we did the air rights transfer. And it was the only way we had the ability to use CNC technology to make that facade; no normal developer would ever have given us that shot. There were no rainscreens in New York, and no one had ever used a laser cutter to make 4,000 facade panels. But the developers agreed because they knew that we were at risk almost more than they were. Only eight years later, that was what got us the Barclays Center project (2012); the client was amazed that we had figured out a way to make that facade. None of this is taught in architecture schools—different structures, different territories, different

David Erdman (left), Gregg Pasquarelli (center), and Michael Maltzan (right) in conversation at Pratt Sessions 7.

responsibilities, different ways of reuse, working around the political and legal system. To me this is what's most exciting about architecture, as long as it ends up in making a building that we want to save and preserve in the future.

Maltzan: I think that's a very important point. It's a capability that architects too often forget they have. They can understand extremely complex and often competing impulses or goals, and they can make sense out of that in a way that still expresses complexity, but moves something forward. That generalist approach to the world is even more powerful now than it was in the past.

For a long time, you couldn't do prefabrication in LA because as soon as you make two of something, the city considers it a product, which has to be specifically approved. That meant that the prefab units were a product and nobody wanted to invest to produce these, which in turn meant that you couldn't access that technology. So, as architects, before we even started making the building, our role was to work with the city to determine how the process of inspection and permitting would work.

Now we're working with the county to develop a pathway for their interest in doing more innovative approaches to affordable housing. There are times when you think you should be running for councilperson, but it is always in the service of this larger project of architecture and urbanism.

Thom Mayne, in the audience: I find it very interesting to see you present and speak together, because Los Angeles and New York are essentially the two centers in the United States that have shared a broader global conceptual thinking. The difference in opportunities is fascinating. Gregg, working in New York your projects are ultimately incredibly simple buildings. They're a bottom, a top, and an extruded thing with stuff in between, but it uses state-of-the-art technology at every level. And in Los Angeles, Michael works with immensely primitive systems. While this primitivism is frightening, he gets to shape things and make much more complicated organizational ideas than you can in New York. What it represents is not a plus or minus, but the difference in opportunities that are offered in different cultures.

Pasquarelli: Well, what happened in New York, in a reaction against modernism in the 1980s, was that the zoning rules changed. There was a tightening of the envelope relative to the floor area ratio, and now the building is prescribed in many ways. The fight is over the last few inches of the facade and a couple moves.

A decade ago, we said to ourselves, "we've got to stop working in New York because we can't play with section." The mantra in the firm became "more section," and we went from having 80 percent of our work in New York City to having only 20 percent here. I'd rather take the primitive system and see what you can do with it.

Erdman: Part of the goal of these talks is to look at geographical areas, and to flip over some of these distinctions. SHoP uses things like the patina, which is not the normal model in New York, whereas Michael's work can be very restrained in its use of color and the very selective use of section in the ground plane. It is nowhere near as unleashed and wild as you might see in earlier work by LA-based architects. There have been such migrations across the coast that the culture you're talking about may be a generational culture. I think these two architects are great because they announced some of the geographical differences in their practices and are in many ways borne out of their cities, but they also open up new ways that don't re-inscribe the LA/New York polarities.

As the density in LA is coming a little closer to New York and Brooklyn is getting a little bit more like LA, those discourses could begin to benefit from each other.

Audience Question: I found it interesting that Michael's talk started with the Weissenhofsiedlung—the idea of the social project in architecture as tied very much to a formal project. The formal and the social were inherently the dual ambition of the modernist project. Gregg's presentation ended with a project that is for the 1 percent in New York. One could say that urban density is essentially a coming together of immense capital. We've come into a new liberal extreme era where we have to confront this, and it's not about the project itself because the work is beautiful. But as architects, how do we build in an age of the 1 percent—a term that didn't even exist 10 years ago?

Pasquarelli: The American Copper Building is 30 percent affordable housing and rental project. 111 West 57th Street is an anomaly, of which only a handful will be built in this city. The value of these super tall towers could be an entire talk, which is about exclusion, racist co-op boards, and financing mechanisms. Obviously, there's a capitalist side, but it's a deeper conversation about a politics of exclusion. We took on the project because we thought it would be interesting. We thought we could do something spectacular and felt the responsibility to make something that was at least as good from the outside as from the inside, because it was going to be built whether we were involved or not.

Erdman: I think this is a wonderful point. Super slender towers could make the city more dense, if it follows the legacy of Hong Kong and we get smaller pencil towers with similar slenderness ratios that accommodate more compact units. If the economy shows a propensity that would align itself with what Hong Kong has done, it's very likely that you start to see more of this. The population of New York is identical to Hong Kong and the land size is almost identical. The difference is that Hong Kong lives on only one third of the area.

The restructuring of cities like New York, London, and Hong Kong is in many ways tethered by trade rules and international finance. The investment that's going into New York, which suggest today that there's going to be more investment from Hong Kong and Asia in New York than there is from North Americans, will lead to property models that are more keen to those that are being developed in Asia, which is why these projects are happening right now.

The first round of these towers isn't adding to quantitative density. It is mostly physical and who knows how it will shake out, but the speculations about that as land use gets more compressed. If you don't want to take over a lot of neighborhoods, the theory would be that you'd have to do more of this, but probably at smaller scales with higher densities in them.

Stan Allen

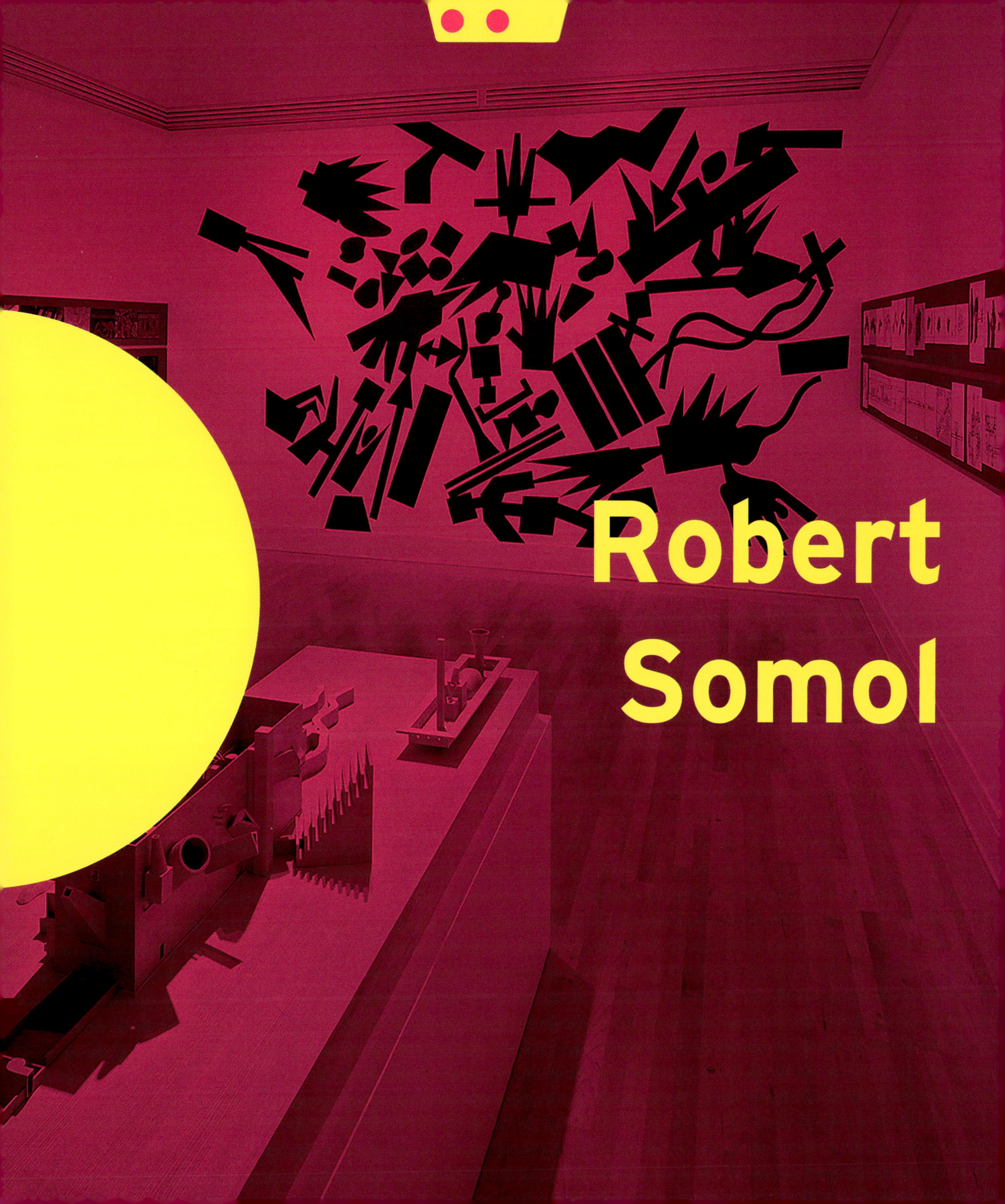

Robert Somol

01

02

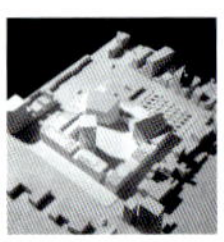

03

04

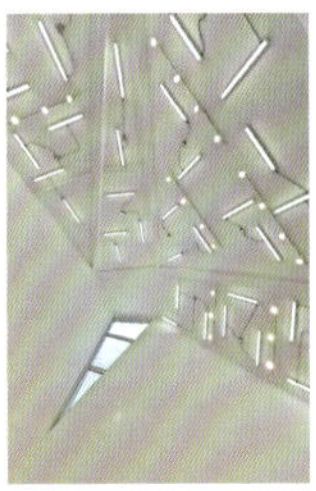

05

06

07

08

09

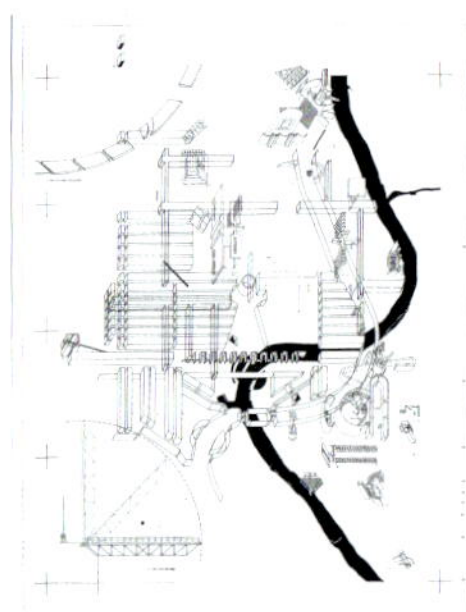

10

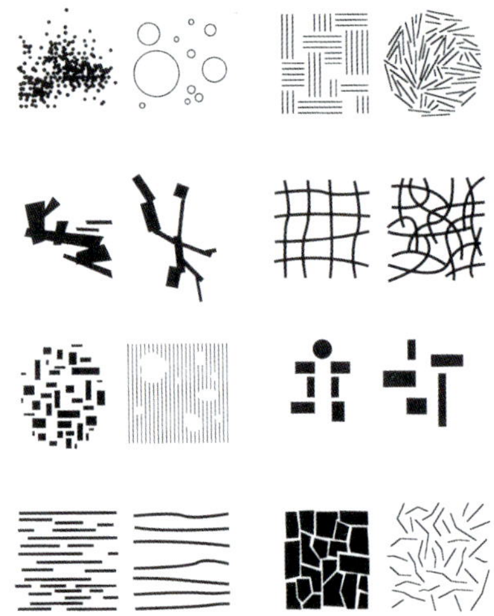

11

12

13

16

18

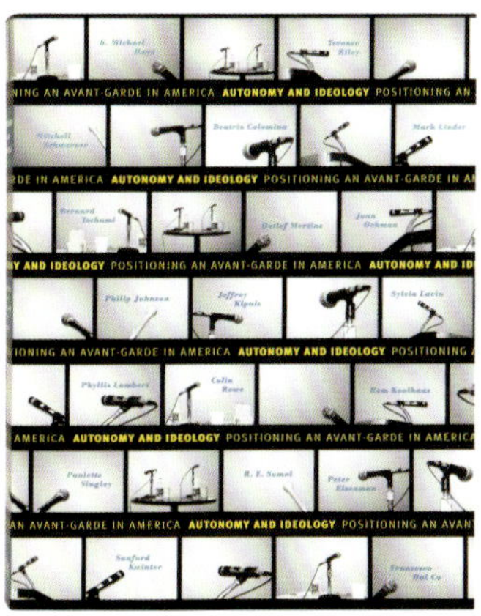

14

15

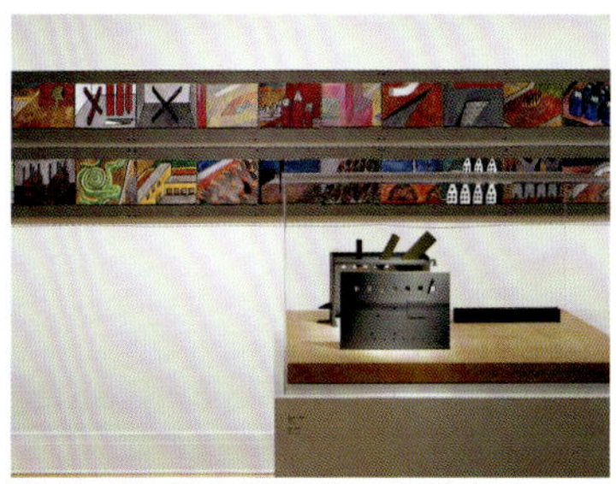

17

19

20

Introduction

DAVID ERDMAN

Robert Somol and Stan Allen are among the most prominent voices to have shaped and attenuated architecture culture over the past decades. One is a practicing architect who writes, and the other is a writer who has practiced. Both are critics with an interest in curation, either explicitly or implicitly through writing, exhibitions, and other initiatives. They both rigorously explore the depths of the discipline, its canons and its various bifurcations. Each has expanded the ways in which we might understand architectural practice, its formats and, its limits, while cumulatively having had a discernible impact on the contemporary culture of education.

As serious as Stan is as a person and how rigorous he is as a thinker, his work relies on a high degree of playfulness. It shifts between a loose arrangement of crystalline parts [01] to those arranged in a frame [02] or dense granular arrays of smaller parts [03] that kaleidoscopically form patches and fields, hatches and points. The scale of the work is diverse, ranging from reflected ceilings to urban gateways.[04] [05] It pushes the limits of cohesion between objects and fields, often times testing their dimensionalities. There is subtlety where elements may collectively vibrate between aggregated parts and sheared planes,[06] or imbue a surface with a degree of plasticity, while operating just within its dimensional modulus of elasticity and flatness. [07] [08]

From early work like the Campo Marzio studies,[09] there's a strong reliance on superposition, which has evolved through points and lines and has been articulated, even more recently, as an interest in the notion of the "loose fit."[10]

The programmatic potentials of the space between the layers seem to be among the agendas; a provisional, if not contingent and playful array of textures, which with there is enough cohesion to form a space of interaction. There is some breathing room between parts, but loose assembly tightens, condenses back together.

It is perhaps between these layers, between the points and lines, that we can begin to formulate the relevance of Stan's work to a discussion on context: where there's a conversational aptitude, existing objects influence new objects and vice-versa. Textures of experience, and interior and exterior are in close proximity but not joined or smoothed out.[11] There's always a gap, allowing each organization to influence the other without erasing or ignoring the assets of its adjacencies. It is no longer apparent what came first. Existing points and lines form relationships to new ones and they might flip.

It is this light touch, acceptance of familiarity without same-ness that could be pertinent to our discussion on context later, and within the framework of the term "influence": more specifically, who influenced who, or what influenced what.

Bob continues to be an important thinker and voice in the discipline of architecture. I like to describe him as the Daniel Lanois of Architecture. Probably few, if any, of you know who Lanois is. However, I presume many of you know the guitar player and singer of U2, The Edge. That name comes from the scratchy, thick, and licks and riffs he is known for in the music industry, and it is arguably what gave U2 its distinctive sound and what skyrocketed the band's popularity starting with the unforgettable *Fire*, which was produced by Brian Eno and Daniel Lanois.

It was Lanois, a guitarist's guitarist, who developed that sound. And like Lanois, I regard Somol as a master architectural wordsmith, who has opened up new narratives that situate the discipline and profession in entirely unimagined ways.

He's been a prolific and consistent voice for decades, starting with his regular appearances in *Assemblage*,[12] where he often appeared alongside Stan, who was the project editor, and in *Any* magazine,[13] founded and edited by Cynthia Davidson, director of Anyone Corp, executive editor of *Log*, and faculty member in the GAUD.

Bob's essays in those journals often alluded to familiar and known phrases outside of academia, like popular songs or lyrics from the likes of Paul Simon and Frank Sinatra, luring the reader into an often rigorously researched inversion of their common understanding of various disciplinary matters.

In his ambient, yet forcible role as introducer, editor, interviewer, critic, and observer, Somol takes familiar work like poetics, diagrams, or the avant-garde and recasts their relevance and contemporaneity.[14] [15] Alongside a close group of colleagues, including Sarah Whiting and Jeff Kipnis, who is in the audience tonight, he altered the course of critical theory and seismically helped to shift it toward the projective.

Against the grain of the neo avant-garde and a desire for novelty, Bob slowly but consistently began building an alternative narrative about the discourse and its future; one which embraces the *familiar*, the *similar*, having a kind of echo or "doppler-like" repetition. Taboo language was foregrounded—*shape* versus form, *cool* versus hot, *easy* versus difficult, *graphic* versus geometry. The ideas were built upon; they were used to reread canons and pair up unlikely bedfellows like Jack Nicholson and Mies van der Rohe.

Bob has collaborated with a number of architects and worked on exhibitions with them, where you can see these modalities have begun to imprint themselves. Take for example the serial bands in John Hejduk's retrospective at the CCA, an exhibition that Bob co-curated. 16 17 Texts and architecture are not oppositional in Bob's world. They are mutual influencers and advocates of one another.

His graphic equalizer, a sorting mechanism that blends word and form, was a mandatory pit stop in the Chicago Biennial last year. 18 In parallel with his directorship at the University of Illinois at Chicago, Bob has become not only an important asset to the culture of Chicago, but the distinct imprint of his cool discourse seems to be popping up all over. It's blunt; it places words in buildings as a form of experiential calligraphy. It turns representations of buildings into words; even going so far as to suggest that language in the spoken word is still alive and a vital aspect of the discourse of the city.

Recent provocations continue to churn up presumed assumptions against the backdrop of the "digital turn" and neo-avant-garde novelty, leaving a distinctive presence of mood. Whether he's acting as a juror or as a member of an editorial board for a magazine (*Flat Out*) that parades graphic flatness and cartoons, where he anonymously appears in cameos, Bob has certainly made an impact. 19 20

By bringing these two amazing minds together for a rare pairing, we might discover something about contexts, perhaps something right in front of our faces. Stan suggested we might use Harold Bloom's *The Anxiety of Influence* (1973) and its more recent counterpart written by Jonathan Lethem, *The Ecstasy of Influence* (2007), as the framework for his and Bob's presentations and ensuing discussion.

I thought it was necessary, if for no other reason than to call out one obvious influence on the discussion of context between Bob and Stan: the issue of the diagram. For which we must thank Cynthia Davidson for foregrounding it 20 years ago in the 1998 issue of *Any*, entitled "Diagram Work," in which both Bob and Stan participated. It goes against the grain of these figures to striate words from form, writing from practice: they do both. They are part of a species of critics who embrace the diagram as a format that bridges content and form.

The diagram's legacy in some ways rests upon the aforementioned looseness. A diagram influences but does not directly illustrate outcomes. The content of the context or a site is provisional in the diagram.

Stan and Bob's essays in "Diagram Work," like the Bloom and Lethem essays, are almost identical mirrors in title, though not directly related. In "Diagrams of Matter," Bob uses the diagram to resolve the dichotomy between form and word, entwining them as equally real or virtual. He situates the diagram as a contemporary counterpart to the desire for a return to the real.

Stan's essay, "Diagrams Matter," situates matter and information as two necessary sides of the provisional, inextricably linking organization, material, form, and content. He promises the diagram as valuable to architecture in so much as one might understand it as a machine of abstraction to speculate on various contexts.

The impact of those conversations revolving around the diagram is evident in the artifacts documenting them as much as they are in the influence their thinking has had on an emerging generation of thinkers and designers. Yet there remains as much anxiety as there is ecstasy about how their different yet related approaches to context, loose and cool, where influences are actively enabled to flourish. A counterpoint to consider, as Jesse Reiser has pointed out, is that while Stan and Bob's understandings of how influence might productively contribute to a discourse of context, we should be wary that those ideas could also be dangerously retrograde, or misconstrued as a nostalgic mode of recovering past ideas of context—something not entirely unfamiliar to recent discussions in various journals.

Needless to say, it is important and a delight to welcome both here this evening to dig into these ideas and explore them together.

Stan Allen

NEW YORK CITY, NY

As David mentioned in his introduction, I put the topic of influence on the table as a basis for discussion tonight. Here the context is the relationship that each individual architect constructs with the legacy of the discipline.

The inevitable starting point for this conversation is the canonical work by Harold Bloom, *The Anxiety of Influence*, published in 1973. In the introduction of the book, Bloom says,

> Poetic history, in this book's argument, is held to be indistinguishable from poetic influence, since strong poets make that history by misreading one another, so as to clear imaginative space for themselves.

This is a very succinct description of what Bloom understands to be this notion of "the anxiety of influence."

From Bloom's often Freudian perspective, if you pretend that anxiety of influence doesn't exist, then you repress it, and of course it comes back to haunt you. Now, Bloom is somebody who believes deeply in the Western canon. He has an idea of the creative artist as a battling hero. Again, he writes,

> My concern is only with strong poets, major figures with the persistence to wrestle with their strong precursors, even to the death. Weaker talents idealize; figures of capable imagination appropriate for themselves.

Picasso said that very succinctly. He said, "Good artists borrow. Great artists steal."

Bloom lays out six different strategies, nuanced discussions of the way in which influence operates. One important strategy to talk about is the notion of clinamen or the idea of misreading, which for Bloom derives from Lucretius's idea of the swerve of the atoms that makes change possible in the universe. It is the idea of an artist swerving from the work of his or her precursor. What Bloom also talks about is that when a younger poet is facing the work of a strong precursor, they don't go for the fully formed mature work. They find some sort of marginal unfinished project; perhaps an early work where the ideas were not fully formed yet, which gives the younger artist a foothold into the work.

The phrase "the anxiety of influence" has entered the critical lexicon. These ideas are very powerful and often resonate with anybody involved in creative work. For somebody of my generation—someone educated under the sign of intertextuality and re-reading, somebody exposed to Roland Barthes and *The Death of the Author*, Jean Baudrillard's discussions about simulation, living through the art world fascination with appropriation in the 1980s—this image of the strong, almost exclusively male figure wrestling with his precursors can begin to seem a little ponderous and dated.

I was certainly prepared to embrace the ideas of Jonathan Lethem. His essay, "The Ecstasy of Influence," was originally published in 2007 with the subtitle "A Plagiarism." At the end of his text, he essentially says, "Well, basically every sentence in his article has been stolen from somewhere else." He goes on to list all of his sources, so it's not strictly plagiarism.

It's a playful work. His references don't come from Milton, Shakespeare, or the King James Bible. They come from William Burroughs, from Bob Dylan, and *The Simpsons*. This essay helped me to position myself between an acceptance and reliance on Bloom but also to update some of those ideas and find a looser, more playful way to approach them.

Both Bloom and Lethem are operating more or less within the world of literature. How can we specifically think about these questions in architecture and the visual arts? For this presentation, I've proposed six categories of my own.

Amnesia: I begin in the sense with the counter category of historical amnesia—forcefully forgetting history, which was so fundamental to early modernism. Consider Hannes Meyer's Co-op Zimmer from 1926. He drafted basically an entire page full of equations and calculations of how he thought architecture should be produced. You want to strip away all reference to the past, all references to the cultural situation of architecture, to start from scratch in this very austere bachelor's room. He provides the list of the things that you need take into account when you're designing a house: 1. sex life, 2. sleeping habits, 3. pets, 4. gardening, 5. personal hygiene, 6. weather protection. I love the fact that it takes him six categories to get to the idea of shelter, and that gardening, pets, and sex life are all more important.

Now, we know that the historical amnesia of the modernist project was actually very incomplete and uneven. A figure like Giuseppe Terragni was very engaged with the past. Colin Rowe described the way in which certain proportional relationships carry through from classical architecture to modern architecture. It's an incomplete picture at best and perhaps doesn't seem terribly productive.

Lateness: A Bloomian category is the notion of lateness. Particularly as it applies to the generation of my teachers, people active in the 1960s, '70s and, '80s primarily. A good example is Le Corbusier's Maisons Jaoul, built in the 1950s outside of Paris, which James Stirling was very interested in. Again, it's not a canonical project by Le Corbusier; it's this kind of marginal project that gives Stirling a foothold for his project for Ham Commons in 1958.

My teacher John Hejduk was very much working through this sense of having come late to the modernist party; that the great innovations of modernism had already taken place 50 years before they started to work. How could they position themselves in relation to this work? In a 1991 interview, Hejduk said outright,

> We're born, you could say, appropriately too late because there's a lot of architects in my generation running around thinking they're masters. A generation before or two generations were masters, I mean real masters of architecture.

He's talking about Mies and Corb but then he says that Corb really should have done a wall house. Now, the wall house belongs to a Corbusian vocabulary. It's moving in a different direction. He says,

> I am like a fly that comes in and says, 'OK, here is one aspect that has been left out, yet which has great potentiality, it should be wrapped up.'

That to me is a very good example of finding this marginal moment and producing something within the logic of the weight of that legacy.

Memory: Of course, there are other architects of that generation who felt that you had to work consciously against the historical amnesia of early modernism. Most prominent is Aldo Rossi, whose work is based on the notion that there are certain collective images of the city. As an architect, not only do you have an imperative to work with that shared collective consciousness, but it's a source of incredible expressive power, as we see in a work like the Modena Cemetery, and that is embedded into the structure of the city itself.

In the 1978 design competition, Roma Interrotta, the use of memory became a bit literal. Twelve international architects were given sections of the Nolli plan and were asked to make fictional interventions, as if the intervening 250 years of history had not happened. That was a kind of reverse amnesia.

Irony + Quotation: In a way, I think you need a little irony in your approach to the past. You need to recognize the distance to the past, and of course irony and quotation were fundamental to a lot of work with postmodernism.

Charles Jencks identified a passage by Umberto Eco, which he said was James Stirling's favorite definition of the postmodern. Eco writes,

> The postmodern reply to the modern consists of recognizing that the past, since it cannot really be destroyed because destruction leads to silence, must be revisited: but with irony, not innocently. I think of the postmodern attitude as that of a man who loves a very cultivated woman and knows that he cannot say to her 'I love you madly,' because he knows that she knows (and that she knows he knows) that these words have already been written by Barbara Cartland.

Now, "Who is Barbara Cartland?" you might ask. She was a British romance novelist. Eco goes on,

> Still, there is a solution. He can say, 'As Barbara Cartland would put it, I love you madly.' At this point, having avoided false innocence, having said clearly that it is no longer possible to speak innocently, he will nevertheless have said what he wanted to say to the woman: that he loves her in an age of lost innocence. If the woman goes along with this, she will have received a declaration of love all the same. Neither of the two speakers will feel innocent, both will have accepted the challenge of the past, of the already said, which cannot be eliminated; both will consciously and with pleasure play the game of irony.

There you have the best definition of postmodernism. It's easy to find flippant examples of this in Stirling's work. In Roma Interrotta, he realized the absurdity of the game, so he quotes himself. In his quadrant of the Nolli plan, he inserts all of his projects to date and it actually makes a pretty reasonable contribution.

Appropriation: Irony can have its limits and the question that was on everybody's mind in the early 1980s, under the influence of Roland Barthes and Baudrillard, was, "What happens if you take the quotation marks away?" If a quotation always takes a fragment and operates according to a logic of fragments, what if you just simply take the entire work?

It questions ideas of authorship and originality. We saw this in Sherrie Levine's reproductions of Walker Evan's Depression-era photographs from 1981, and Robert Rauschenberg's "Erased De Kooning Drawing," which is a remarkable work where De Kooning was completely in on the game. Rauschenberg went to De Kooning and asked for a drawing; it took Rauschenberg four days to erase the De Kooning drawing.

For architecture, this is a complicated question. Conditions of authorship are different in architecture than they are in art. In the rebuilding of the Barcelona Pavilion, which had only been known in photography for such a long period of time, what is the status of the new building?

Andres Jaque has tried to call attention to the status of the reconstruction as a kind of simulacrum by bringing all of the cleaning equipment from the basement up and putting it on display as a way to say, "This is what's required in order to maintain the image of that building from 1929." We live now in an era in which the culture of the copy is so ubiquitous that these questions are really changing a lot.

Seamless: My final category relates to Jesús Vassallo's book, *Seamless: Digital Collage and Dirty Realism and Contemporary Architecture* (2016). The book describes what Vassallo understands to be at stake for architecture dealing with this contemporary culture of digital photography and the way in which architecture is continually positioned in relation to image culture.

Vassallo looks at various younger European practices, all of whom have worked very closely with photographers. For my generation, educated by people like John Hejduk, the protagonist in questions of representation was always painting, but I think today the protagonist is photography or digital photography.

We tend to think of photography as part of a generalized image culture that is detaching us from that reality, but Vassallo sees it as a way to engage with that world, but through a necessary filter of abstraction. I think it's a productive and interesting argument.

To wrap up, if I were to generalize what I think is at stake here, it has to do with the conversational model of the discipline. In order to have a good conversation, first of all, you need to speak the same language; not only a shared language in verbal terms, but a shared language in terms of the way you function and operate in the discipline. You also have to share a common set of references and your history.

There has to be a general agreement as to what the issues are that matter, and you have to agree that those issues fall within the scope of your disciplinary expertise. There's a tendency in a lot of schools to be seduced by things like climate change and the refugee crisis in Europe. Nobody is saying that those are not urgent issues, but they're not issues in which architecture actually has a lot of discipline.

Then, within those fairly simple set of conditions, you can also disagree because part of a conversation is having an argument, the traction of different points of view.

It also means that the discipline moves forward precisely by this kind of internal conversation. You begin by acknowledging that the discipline has already answered certain questions, and you don't have to start from scratch every time you start a new project. In fact, by acknowledging the work that has been done before, you actually have a better chance of doing something new.

Finally, I would say, certainly in the context of architectural education, that education is all about the anxiety of influence. It's a conversational enterprise and it's completely bound up with these questions.

Robert Somol

CHICAGO, IL

Stanley Tigerman, *The Titanic*, 1978

As someone once said, "Everything that needs to be said has been said already, just not yet by everybody who needs to say it." I will now repeat everything that was just said by esteemed friends, Stan and David. I want to thank Stan, who has been my long-term fellow traveler, for subpoenaing me to testify with him in these proceedings this evening, because I do think we have some things to answer for in public.

About 20 years ago, Stan and I, with others in our roughly identifiable generation, initiated a dispute with some forms of the dominant critical academic regimes that we were born under, starting with our participation in the conference that was organized by Joan Ockman called *Things in the Making*. It developed variously through an investment in conditions, operations, performance, doing, practice, the projective, et cetera.

Given what has passed as architecture over the last decade, which has seemed to stem from some of those developments, I think it's time that we reassess in public or at least reassert more directly.

I've given my presentation today the title "Somewhere Down There: Contexts, Characters, Conditions, Conceits." I think that today, conditions have captured conceits and that for me ultimately architecture is in the conceit business and not in the condition business. As for the primary title, it relates to a conference that was held at UIC in 1985. There was an exchange about Rem Koolhaas's Villa Dall'Ava (1991) in which Michael Graves references Le Corbusier's Casa Guruchet (1953) as a precedent. He says, "Rem, there's a house—I've been trying to remember its name. I think it's in Chile." Peter Eisenman follows, "It's in Brazil." Mario Gandelsonas says, "It's in Argentina." And Peter Eisenman concludes. "It's south of the border, somewhere down there."

It's easy to laugh at this, across the geo-ethnocentrism, whether we laugh out of superiority or outrage. But I want us to question that too-quick response, which is merely the fallout of our own global, neoliberal discourse. Today, between GPS, Google Earth, Wikipedia, and Siri, we can basically locate any stick ever erected by humans anywhere on earth within a meter. So, a project's location is not that interesting. In fact, I think in some sense, it is totally uninteresting. What is very interesting though is that we have a generation interested in identity—where things are but not so much what the significance of it is.

Despite not knowing where this house by Le Corbusier was, I think Michael Graves was incredibly insightful for bringing up this project as a precedent relative to Villa Dall'Ava. Separated by 40 years, 7,000 miles, and across two hemispheres, Corb is the context for OMA. In other words, context is an architectural conceit. The possibilities for architecture to understand, confront, engage, or reconstruct context is an architectural possibility first.

There are two images by Stanley Tigerman—*The Titanic* from 1978 and *The Epiphany* from 2015; a photomontage and a digital collage, respectively. Today, we routinely talk about context as constructed by flows—material flows or economic, energy flows. In our new materialism, we've lost interest in influence that is literally what flows into and that's the context again. Obviously, Mies is the context for the 1978 image, which shows his Crown Hall sinking into Lake Michigan.

In a way, Stanley is appropriating a Mies technique to undermine Mies, or the School of Mies. It was not really an attack on Mies but an attempt to save Mies from his acolytes and disciples. *The Titanic* represents the ship that launched a thousand faces. While *The Titanic* announces the end of a movement or a singular modernism, it simultaneously gives birth to the proliferation of personalities in its wake.

Almost 40 years after *The Titanic*, in its own legacy of influence and repetition, Stanley was invited to revisit himself by updating his image. In its 2015 sequel, the *The Epiphany*, Crown Hall is apparently saved and now fills half the horizon, shared with its unlikely partner, Frank Gehry's Guggenheim

Stanley Tigerman, *The Epiphany*, Stanley Tigerman, 2015

Bilbao (1997). Both buildings are abandoned on an arid, alien landscape, beneath the same cumulus-filled sky over Lake Michigan. Streaking down the center of the view is what looks to be a bomb, positioned above the overlap of the two buildings, its exhaust plume ripping the image exactly in half. The falling object, recalling Newton's epiphany with the apple, structures the art historical duality of the image. The pristine rectangle of glass and steel stands in contrast to the pyramidal pile of torqued titanium; the former actually suspended, while the latter only appears to challenge gravity.

Made so many years apart, these projects suggest two distinct architectural worlds; the culmination of one thing and the beginning of another. But the formal juxtaposition also makes evident the classical symmetry of both projects, each with tripartite frontal divisions whose central bay serves as a monumental entrance; the projecting podium of the one echoed in the colossal canopy of the other. With Guggenheim and Crown Hall sized evenly to fill the horizon, *The Epiphany* conceals the fact that the area of Bilbao was actually ten times the size of IIT's primary volume. The twin icons, now rendered equivalent in the wake of 9/11; Mies transformed into a starchitect *avant la lettre*, before both awaiting similar fates in the desert.

Falling exactly at the midpoint of this 40-year period between Mies and Gehry would be Tigerman's own original explosive, *The Titanic*. It is what connects and separates these conjoined twins, a surrogate for the paper age of architecture generally, from the late 1950s to the mid-'90s, an interregnum missing from that image except perhaps as embodied by that cartoonish grenade. It's noteworthy that in *The Titanic* the agency of disaster is invisible. It's unclear as to whether its causes are natural or human-made, iceberg or torpedo, or perhaps more likely, modernism simply sinking of its own weight, its own hubris even in the dead calm of Lake Michigan.

To the contrary, agency is configured dead center in *The Epiphany*. It's the M-69 from World War II, which is about 8 inches big, and therefore clearly in the foreground. Moreover, it was only used during training and is totally inert. Both in terms of where it is and what it is, no explosion is possible.

Given the fact that *The Epiphany* is a digital collage, all elements are easily findable if you surf the web. In a certain sense, the context of the second image is really that virtual archive as much as it is something else. The 1978 photomontage uses the model of Crown Hall submerging in a sea of reality. The 2015 Photoshop rendering presents the actual building. In other words, in 1978 the most real part of the image is the context, the view of Lake Michigan that accounts for 90 percent of the surface area of the original. In 2015, the most real thing is two built structures that firmly hold the datum.

What sunk as representation or idea in 1978 is resurrected as fact in 2015. Or to put it another way, what died as ideology—modernism—returns now as identity, whether produced by the object or the subject, the icon or the starchitect. This is confirmed by the transition implied by the titles, *The Titanic* to *The Epiphany*, charting a trajectory from a collective catastrophe to a personal experience.

While *The Epiphany* beautifully captures the current preoccupation with identity, the abstract and evacuated context to the image suggest that its proffered lesson would advance merely another identity.

The problem Tigerman suggests is with a particular delimited identity—that of the icon or that of the starchitect—that has been removed from its context. The remedy, it seems, is merely a greater recognition of the actual site. You could say it's a double-down on reality, the redundancy of putting the real back into the real.

To shift from the two Mieses and the two Stanleys to the two Bonds: we can see a similar shift from ideology to identity in James Bond movies from roughly the same period. What was great about the early James Bond was that he was a boring functionary of the state. He was always all business and all pleasure. The new Bond on the other hand, Daniel Craig, is quietly tortured and almost is never on the clock. They can never locate him because there is no real job to do anymore after the Cold War. He's really always on a personal mission of revenge or retribution.

Recent Bond movies, like *Skyfall* (2012) or *Spectre* (2015), always include scenes with the villain, where Bond is tied up and they're having some kind of psychotherapy session with him. The story lines are no longer about ideological warfare, but about personal epiphanies and stories of identity.

For me, this summarizes *The Titanic* and *The Epiphany*: the collective catastrophe versus the personal experience; the photomontage versus Photoshop; the model/idea versus the actual building in its reality; the issue of a moment of ideology and disagreement versus identity and empathy; a moment from authors and arguments to agents and research; from saying as a form of marking intent to doing as measuring impact; and conceits versus conditions.

In relation to the two Tigerman images and the two Bonds, as a final pairing we can look at the two maps of contemporary postwar architectural practices. One is the famous Charles Jencks image of 1971; the other is the Alejandro Zaera-Polo version of 2016. The Jencks model is interesting because you have to understand the context of the 1970s, which is right of the midpoint of this map, depicting 70 years before it and another 30 years into the future. It is a projective version of history. For Jencks, it comes out of a series of ideological or structured ideas and dichotomies that unfold over time and emerge in different combinations, so that it can plot out the future of architecture, not merely its past.

Zaera Polo's map shows only 2016. It is a snapshot of the here and now; there is no past, there is no future, there's no genealogy, no legacy, no anxiety of influence. There is just a set of practices, which precede any ideas.

Jencks's image is filled with gaps, whereas Alejandro's only has overlaps. For me, one of the important aspects of how one maintains the possibility of a "Project"—over and against having a practice—is the way in which you have to maintain the gap between representation and reality, word and image, ambition, and ability.

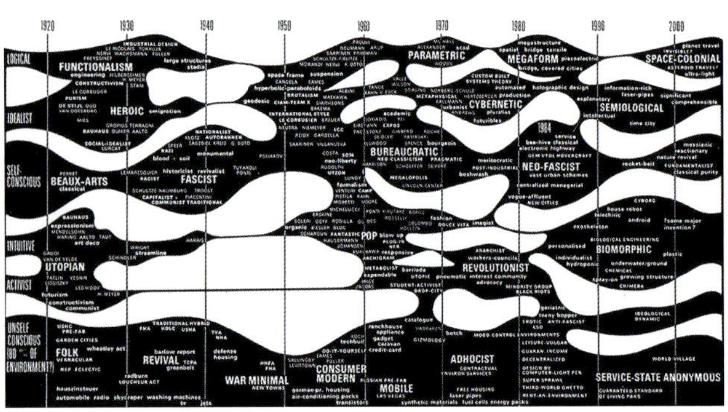

Charles Jencks, *Evolutionary Tree to the Year 2000* (revision), 2000 (original drawing from 1971)

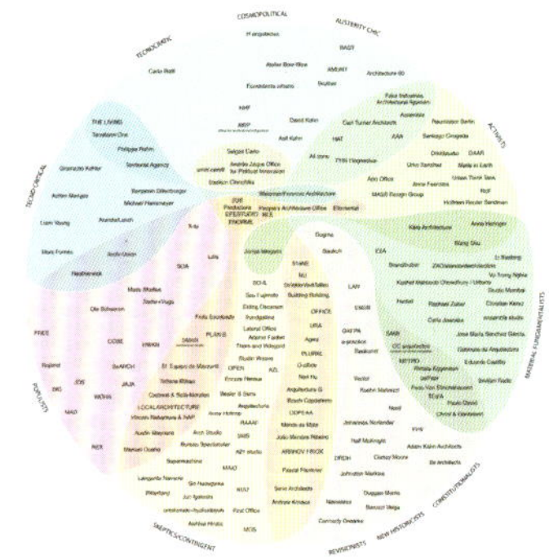

Alejandro Zaera Polo, *Political Compass: A Taxonomy of Emerging Architecture in One Diagram*, 2016

The possibility of a Project in architecture has historically occupied the gap between ambition and ability. But we've come to a moment where our ambitions have slackened and our abilities have intensified or exaggerated such that now we have the exact point of intersection, where our ambitions and our abilities are perfectly isomorphic and mapped on to each other. In other words, this is the culture of doing. Maybe that dot is what we call practice.

Doing becomes self-evidently isomorphic to intent. Doing becomes its own justification. This also focuses on our current preoccupation with means, techniques, mediums, practices; the fixation on office structure, on delivery, and on delivery models guaranteed by BIM and other softwares.

The explosion of practice as a word has come to replace discipline. It's not "architecture"; we are now doing special practice, integrated practice, cultural practice, discursive practice, or curatorial practice. The proliferation of practice is also part of that techno-anthropologicalization of our field, keeping our discipline at arm's length, which is tied to a certain contemporaneity of metric models of evaluation, core competencies, and so on.

In Zaera Polo's map, 2016 eliminates the ability to project; it reduces us to flatten down the here and now. There is no escaping the here and now; it forecloses us both from a past and a future.

This is a problem I have with the idea of resiliency, the cliché *du jour*, which is interested in only maintaining the current, the perpetuation of the system; the "here and now" as if it were forever adequate and doable. Resilience replaces those other temporalities, whether it's the extreme modernist erase-and-replace version of the future, or postmodernist preservation: the maintenance of the archaic.

For all of their opposition or perhaps because of the oppositions between modern and postmodern, they were both positions with ideologies. They had a view about how to move forward. They set out values. Each position had a dispute with the present and a projective way of going elsewhere. Resilience is post-ideological and basically models a compromise, where nothing is ever really new and nothing is ever really worth preserving. That is the new context that we inhabit—a continuously updated version of the "here and now," which is merely a set of dashboards and models.

Conversation

STAN ALLEN AND ROBERT SOMOL

Catherine Ingraham, in the audience: In thinking about *The Anxiety of Influence* and the reworking of the past and the present—how some precedent is still absolutely necessary in some way, even if you treat it as a trivial influence—I was reminded of Francis Bacon, a painter who used the diagram very specifically as a way of wrestling with past portraiture artists. He wanted to paint portraiture, but it was out of his time to do so. He started to mess around with the paint diagrammatically as a way of working through the problem of portraiture in his time. With that, he ended up really breaking into the skin of the person by finding the forces underneath. That would have been a violent thing to do. I'm curious about whether there's an element of violence or friction in that passage.

Stan Allen: I think it is important to hold onto the difficulty and the tension that's implied. It's not simply a vassal play with an all-accessible past. As Bob presented, even in the passage from 1978 to 1997, things changed; what it means to have some reference and access to the past has changed. I don't know that it's a question of going back to a model of resistance or slowness, but the dominant model is about speed, quickness, and total accessibility. I think you do have to push back on that.

Robert Somol: For me, it is about how we can imagine a different future than one that is just extrapolated from present concerns. This is why I wanted our presentations tonight to be a bit of a "mea culpa." There was that moment in the mid- to late '90s, when a different agenda arose. It was an important moment, but things got lost in translation. So, part of it is to become a corrective to going off the tracks. In terms of Stan's work, I think infrastructuralism was a really interesting idea because it was sort of impossible. Post 2008, what that becomes for another generation is, "Let's do bridge repair," and I don't know where the Project is anymore. In infrastructuralism, the ambition and the ability were at a gap. Today, they basically become identical.

Allen: Or the reverse of that. I think that's your point about ambitions and abilities—there's no longer a gap. Something impossible, like building a city for two million people from scratch, is not actually impossible at all. In fact, it's happening in places like China.

Jeff Kipnis, in the audience: Fiction, commentary, and criticism were things that Bob championed as the vehicles for the last decade. Even though he said a lot of new things tonight, they are still the main vehicles. Fiction is the idiom, and the magazine and the characters are vehicles.

As Stan showed, we're starting to see various forms of actualities of architecture. There's still a building, but there are photographs of the building, and then there's the collaboration between the photographs and the building as other possible realities. Many actualities are put into play. We see a move away from fiction because it leaves in place the possibility that there is a reality.

It has always been a problem to try to transpose fiction and non-fiction from literary rhetoric into architecture, when architecture has always been incarnating a fictionality as its essence of reality. Tonight, it became really clear that legacy is still left over from Bob's brilliant moment, and that it was the commentary to criticism and the vehicle of discussing fiction and non-fiction.

Somol: In that sense, we didn't produce an apostasy, really. This goes back to Barbara Johnson's view that deconstruction is "to put surprise to work." That's my interest and it also comes out of Roberto Unger's ideas of political plasticity. But the question is, how do you de-realize the thing that you think is stable, when it's really not stable? Some architectures do that at some times better than other times. Sometimes they don't do it and then later on, they do it. Those situations change how you put surprise to work, how you put fiction to work, or how you expose the plasticity.

Kipnis: We understand these ideas and how they work in many different disciplines. But as Stan asked, how do we put this to work in architecture? The apotheosis I had recently is that architecture begins its life in many of these cases as already accomplished as fiction. Bob, you talked about all these characters that are already existing in a certain sense. In other words, no one has to be a *dramatis personae* in architecture because everyone in a building or in a program is in character. There is a real difficulty of trying to transport the analysis and the theorization. What we actually need now are new forms of analysis, rather than new forms of criticism.

Allen: With Catherine's description of Francis Bacon working in part through the medium itself, you come to this complicated question, "What is architecture's medium?" I do argue for the irreducibility of built architecture; not because the building is proof of the real expression of architectural ideas but precisely because of its capacity to trigger complex effects that are beyond the drawing, the model, and the rendering.

At the same time, the building can't be the whole story, especially today when the image is the building that circulates. In his work about the reproduction of the Barcelona Pavilion, Andres Jaque is unmasking it as fiction, but it's also killing the possibility of telling more stories, other than the story of the unmasking.

It doesn't particularly bother me that there is a basement with cleaning equipment under the Barcelona Pavilion. That's not consequential to my experience of the building. When I went to visit the Barcelona Pavilion, it was closed for a photo shoot. Of course, it's a great backdrop for a photo shoot, and to me, that's fine. I don't see that as diminishing the greatness of Mies or trivializing his work. It's one among many of the possible stories you could tell about the Barcelona Pavilion.

So, how do we put this to work in architecture? I think it has to do with understanding architecture as something that doesn't just happen through one medium. It happens through many different mediums simultaneously.

David Erdman: I think the examples of buildings that look like photographic effects, or flips where existing buildings

David Erdman (left), Stan Allen (center), and Robert Somol (right) in conversation at Pratt Sessions 11.

become the new building, are weird ways in which the fiction becomes a reality. They circulate back on themselves. I could look at the way Bob has worked on certain disciplinary issues and you pointed it out in the relationship of Rem's project to Le Corbusier or Peter Eisenman's work to Giuseppe Terragni; it can no longer be understood as just that which was there initially but is immediately given a different trajectory. As a way of understanding it, they're producing a fiction that wasn't there prior. Would that be fair to say?

Allen: I would again mention Jesús Vassallo and his counter-intuitive thesis about the role of photography today as not continuous with image culture but as a privilege to the real. He curated a show within the 2017 Chicago Biennial called *A Love of the World*. A lot of the photographs he chose were very tightly cropped images of material. We tend to think of photography as complicit in the idea of object building, but these were not photographs of buildings as objects. They were about surface and texture. You couldn't isolate the building as artifact in those photographs. In a way, I think the answer is not to hold image culture at arm's length but to dive deeper into it.

Image culture is complex and diverse. There might be answers found within that diversity of image culture, if we don't simply dismiss the image because it's ephemeral, and because it circulates on the Internet and creates atmosphere spectacle.

Somol: Nothing I said was meant to undermine the potential radicality of engaging with the fluctuation between matter and image in a project. I think that's one of the gaps that you can activate and reconfigure. But I don't see the ambition to occupy and re-arrange that discrepancy in a lot of recent work. If I'm nostalgic for something, it's the Project and I find that my colleagues and successors have abandoned the idea of the possibility of a Project in architecture.

Audience question: In 1982, the first *Blade Runner* showed the replicas figuring out they are replicas, they're not human. In the new *Blade Runner* (2017), we can see that the replicas tried to establish themselves as a race. If we assume that the humans are real and the replicas are fake, how do we define image, which show us the challenge between the fake and real? How do you define the difference between the original and the image?

Somol: This is going to be a very oblique set of associations from your question but it goes back to an interview that Jeff Kipnis had with Jacques Herzog, in which he relates his relationship to Aldo Rossi. Herzog says, "Rossi interested us in images, but we were never interested in his images, never interested in collecting images of architectural memories." Perhaps this is Herzog & de Meuron's dispute with the predecessor, which they set up and then moved away from. In particular, the way that they think about the image, I think they have a complicated relationship to the Project. Some may believe that they represent the end of the Project because they return to building. But I think they continue the Project in a new height and form.

The excuse of saying, "they killed the Project in favor of the building," is it allows you to brush your hands and say, "Thank God, we're done with the Project and we'll now go off to do something else."

I don't think that's the lesson of Herzog & de Meuron. I think part of it is because of the way in which they keep the reopening the gap between matter and image in physical form. Many practices play the image-game in one medium and play the matter-game in another medium—specifying media as a way to deal with the issues as opposed to trying to conflate them.

Erdman: Those are also not replicas or copies. You can see photographic effects in Herzog & de Meuron's work, but there's no photograph that they're duplicating.

Somol: As I said, they're not considered images for representational purpose.

Audience question: What Bob was saying sparks a few thoughts about his definition of the Project, where the Project lies in the gap between ability and aspirations. Do you think that this generation of people forming all of the different practices or offices is lacking aspirations and maybe hiding under the veil of some indifference? Are they distancing themselves from the older generation in order to produce new architectures that they don't want to define?

Somol: I believe I am the inventor of the indifferent project and I think it's been misappropriated by many people. I think it comes out of pragmatism, which is why I feel a little bit that doing ultimately became its own justification.

Techniques started to appear where that seemed feasible. I do think it is this industrious specialist that I feel have followed us as opposed to lazy generalist that I consider myself. "Doing" was never such a big deal.

Allen: I may be little more optimistic than Bob is. I think there's actually a lot of interesting work going on out there. I wrote this piece called "Practice vs. Project" where I actually argue on the side of practice. What for me is left out of that description and maybe is missing a little bit in some of this contemporary work is the practice model. What gives consistency is actually the discipline itself. In other words, you don't need an articulated Project to assign consistency to the work over time. You rely on the discipline itself to provide consistency. I would say in the positive sense, a lot of these younger practices in fact are engaging questions of disciplinarity.

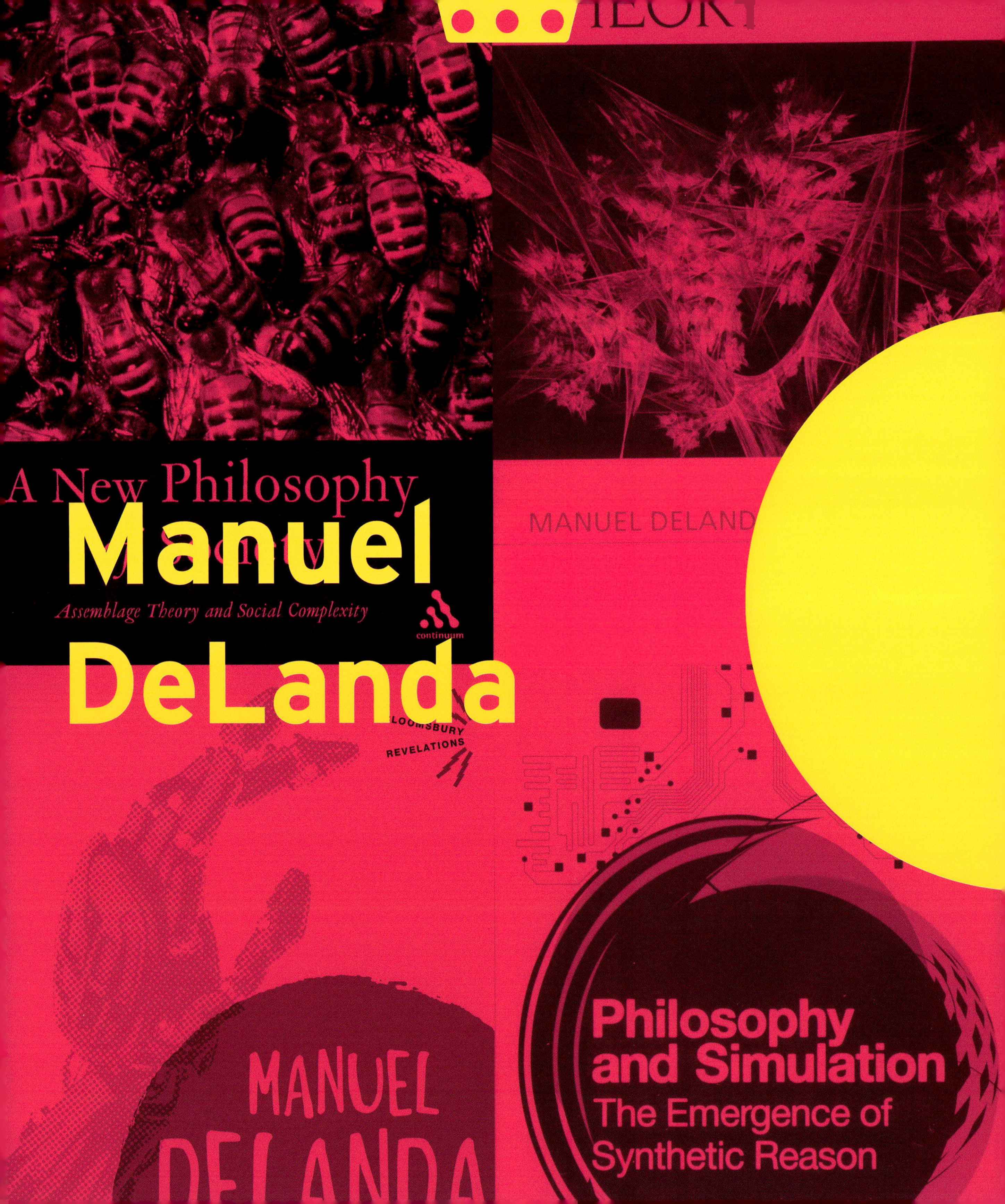

Manuel
DeLanda
A New Philosophy
Assemblage Theory and Social Complexity
continuum
REVELATIONS
MANUEL
Philosophy
and Simulation
The Emergence of
Synthetic Reason

Graham
Harman
books
Dante's
BROKEN HAMMER
THE
OBJECT
GRAHAM HARMAN
Immaterialism
Graham Harman
Networks
Bruno Latour and
Metaphysics

04

01

ZONE
A Serial Publication of Ideas in Contemporary Culture

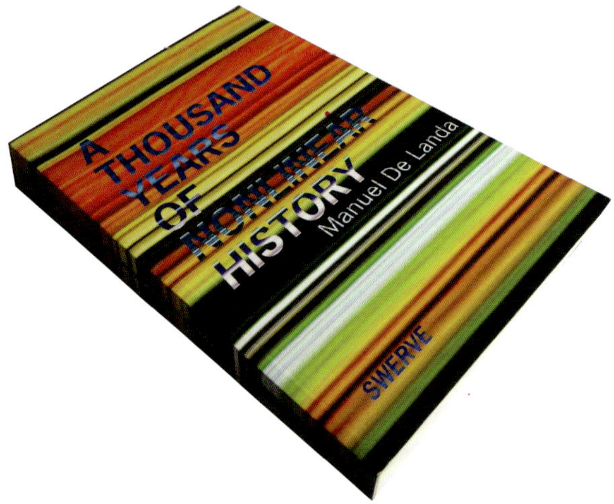
A THOUSAND YEARS OF
HISTORY
Manuel De Landa
SWERVE

Incorporations
Edited by Jonathan Crary and Sanford Kwinter

02

War in the Age of Intelligent Machines
Manuel De Landa
Swerve Editions

03

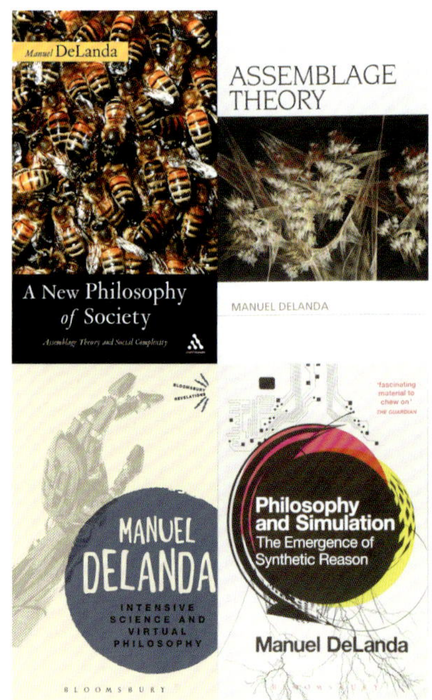
Manuel DeLanda
A New Philosophy of Society
Assemblage Theory and Social Complexity
ASSEMBLAGE THEORY
MANUEL DELANDA
MANUEL DELANDA
INTENSIVE SCIENCE AND VIRTUAL PHILOSOPHY
BLOOMSBURY
'fascinating material to chew on' THE GUARDIAN
Philosophy and Simulation
The Emergence of Synthetic Reason
Manuel DeLanda

05

07

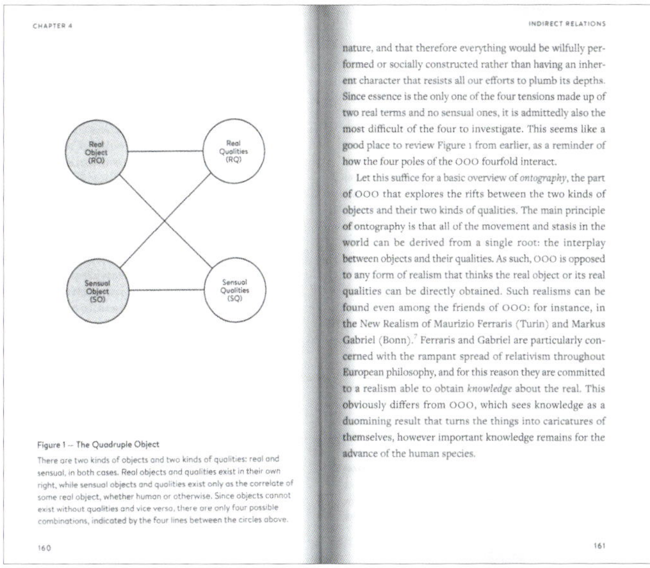

Figure 1 -- The Quadruple Object

There are two kinds of objects and two kinds of qualities: real and sensual, in both cases. Real objects and qualities exist in their own right, while sensual objects and qualities exist only as the correlate of some real object, whether human or otherwise. Since objects cannot exist without qualities and vice versa, there are only four possible combinations, indicated by the four lines between the circles above.

160

INDIRECT RELATIONS

nature, and that therefore everything would be wilfully performed or socially constructed rather than having an inherent character that resists all our efforts to plumb its depths. Since essence is the only one of the four tensions made up of two real terms and no sensual ones, it is admittedly also the most difficult of the four to investigate. This seems like a good place to review Figure 1 from earlier, as a reminder of how the four poles of the OOO fourfold interact.

Let this suffice for a basic overview of *ontography*, the part of OOO that explores the rifts between the two kinds of objects and their two kinds of qualities. The main principle of ontography is that all of the movement and stasis in the world can be derived from a single root: the interplay between objects and their qualities. As such, OOO is opposed to any form of realism that thinks the real object or its real qualities can be directly obtained. Such realisms can be found even among the friends of OOO: for instance, in the New Realism of Maurizio Ferraris (Turin) and Markus Gabriel (Bonn).[7] Ferraris and Gabriel are particularly concerned with the rampant spread of relativism throughout European philosophy, and for this reason they are committed to a realism able to obtain *knowledge* about the real. This obviously differs from OOO, which sees knowledge as a duomining result that turns the things into caricatures of themselves, however important knowledge remains for the advance of the human species.

161

09

11

06

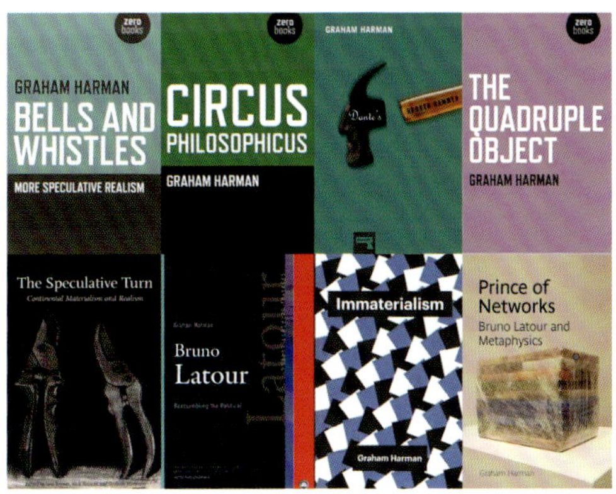

08

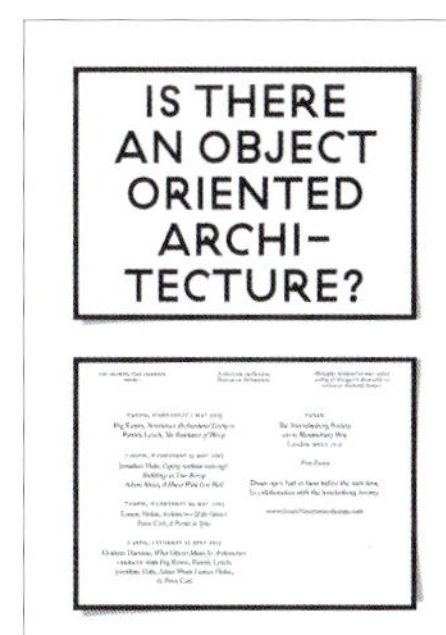

10

Introduction

DAVID ERDMAN

It's an honor to be able to bring together these two incredible minds, Manuel DeLanda and Graham Harman. We're equally delighted that Ferda Kolatan has generously agreed to moderate their discussion.

Graham and Manuel are heavy-hitting forces in the world of philosophy. They construct and reconstruct the ways in which we understand, experience, and think about the world, allowing us to imagine things we don't know or can't see. To this extent, philosophy has historically been an invaluable counterpart to the discipline of architecture. Part of the conversation between the two disciplines is about how objects and their associative qualities, and how the flows and systems that comprise our surrounding environment may develop variegated and productive understandings of the contexts upon which we speculate and build.

Both Graham and Manuel have uprooted their discipline. As much as they are lofty and philosophical, they are also ardent realists. For them there is a world of material flows and objects that exists independently of our minds. Most continental philosophy, rooted largely in Europe, suggests that the world only exists in our minds and because of our ideas, otherwise known as "idealism."

Realism lives one side of *The Matrix* (yes, like the movie) with some "withdrawn" and indirect access to the other side. This is profound in relation to continental philosophy and idealism which lives solely on one side; *it's all in your head*. Flesh, matter, and objects are *not* reality. This is indeed a provocative, charged debate within philosophy. While Graham and Manuel's work has been and continues to be invaluable to architectural thinking and discourse, it is important to recognize and maintain disciplinary boundaries; realizing that much of their work is driven by acute issues within philosophy.

Manuel's interest in energy flows, networks, and matter may stem directly from his personal, raw energy. He is always emphatic, passionate, and pointed. Students line up to attend his lectures and hear him speak. The interest in Manuel, I think, has as much to do with the medium as the content, which largely is Manuel himself. An orator par excellence and an insatiably curious mind, Manuel seems to contradict the laws of thermodynamics, as if there's more energy in his body then its allowable capacity.

He has had a significant impact on the architecture scene. Over 30 years ago, he splashed into it with his essays and books, initially purveyed almost exclusively via the *Zone* imprint. *Zone* was edited by Sanford Kwinter and Jonathan Crary, and designed by Bruce Mau, who also edited a number of *Zone* books, including both of Manuel's volumes. The books were beautiful, well-curated, intellectually stimulating, and visually-compelling objects that brought together a wide array of praxes, including philosophy. One could probably attribute the rise in popularity of continental philosophy in graduate architecture schools in the late 1990s in large part to *Zone*.

At that time, architecture was among several disciplines that were wrestling with the digital turn, and where DeLanda's words and wild riffs on the flows in the Second Machine Age drew attention. *Zone*'s oeuvre is indeed a particular collection of continental philosophy, where DeLanda is in good company among several of his heroes like Deleuze and Bergson. DeLanda was part of the first and final *Zone* compendiums, book-ending the collection. *Zone 1/2: The Contemporary City* [01] included his essay, "Policing the Spectrum," a prelude to his book, *War in the Age of Intelligent Machines* (1991); and "Non-Organic Life," which appeared in *Zone 6: Incorporations*. [02]

War in the Age of Intelligent Machines was an important book as the military industrial complex was seeping into everyday culture; the Internet was becoming available, machinery of surveillance was becoming ever-more present, and computers becoming more personal. *War in the Age of Intelligent Machines* shocked and awed, resonating with issues pertinent to the contemporary human or "post-human" condition. [03]

Looking at a range of subjects from military weaponry to artificial intelligence and new forms of inorganic life, the book primed design and architecture culture as it ushered in the beginning of the Second Machine Age. It heightened our awareness of things we're witnessing today. The book took things that were very abstract and gave them a material palpability or a reality. They were so real in many ways, they became quite horrific.

Manuel's book *A Thousand Years of Non-Linear History* (2003), paying homage to Deleuze's highly acclaimed book *A Thousand Plateaus* (1987), struck a deep cord in architecture culture and discourse by overturning the semiological models of architecture and context that the discipline had fashioned itself on for decades.[04] Presenting three non-linear micro-histories, the book allowed architects to consider the material aspects and outcomes of network flows, their distributions and singularities in urban, rural, geological, human, and planetary situations.

In the framework of our examination of new architectural contexts, one of the most important things about Manuel's brilliant work is that while it emphasizes flows and networks, meshworks, abstract and virtual machines, bottom-up and tactical thinking, it does not suggest that those precede material outcomes; rather they are simultaneously bound up with them.[05]

Graham Harman has been a force in philosophy where he's partly responsible for opening up a rift in the discipline that moves away from its traditions and idealism in continental philosoph; by effectively killing Emmanuel Kant. His world is comprised of discrete objects, not systems and the relational linkages between them.[06] All objects are to be given equal attention. There's no taxonomic hierarchy between humans and nature, real and fictional. And while each object is different, they have a tense relationship with their properties or qualities allowing for change.[07] Graham's realism is an incomplete one and it is mysterious, weird, and unknowable in a way that we can never connect with. It's detached and independent from humanity.

In a relatively short time, Graham has been immensely prolific.[08] One of the distinctive things about his work is that he tests out his ideas and puts his philosophy to work in his writing. He's tried a few worthy and courageous experiments that resulted in spellbinding books where there are plots that oscillate between fiction, nonfiction, narrative commentary, and storytelling while simultaneously evoking deep disciplinary themes. It distinguishes his work from the dry scientific tomes of thick pulp, which have been normalized as philosophy's preferred vehicle of communication. Circuses, myths, monsters, princes, and wolves insinuate a mysterious and strange world we can only partly be in touch with. The gap between objects and qualities is a territory of vast imaginative opportunity in Harman's work.

At the University of London in April 2007, Graham Harman, Quentin Meillassoux, Ray Brassier, and Iain Hamilton Grant stunned the philosophical community with the introduction of Speculative Realism.[09] It is the umbrella philosophy that includes Harman's "Triple O," formally known as Object-Oriented Ontology. It is important to realize that over those same dates in 2007, Graham spent an entire day at the Architectural Association on reviews and delivering a lecture. In this way, Graham is not only one of the most prominent philosophers to move the discourse away from Europe, but also possibly the first whose work is interacting with architectural discourse at the same time it is forming. His contributions to *Tarp* (the GAUD student journal) and *Log* paralleled and ratified Triple O at a moment that architectural discourse was also taking on new form and lines of inquiry.

The indirect relations or gaps that Graham identifies in Triple O between types of objects and their qualities has sparked a discourse in architecture around the term "estrangement" and reintroduced an interest in coarseness, edge, boundary, and thickness against the backdrop of edgeless, light, smooth topologies. While the impact of this thinking on architectural education is just starting to take root and winding debate in the discourse, we're just beginning to test and discover the potentials of Triple O in architecture.[10]

Graham and Manuel were brought together this evening in part because of their recently co-authored book, *The Rise of Realism* (2017).[11] Conversational in tone and immensely engaging, it is the first explicit accounting of the differences and similarities between their philosophies. It jumps right in, as if you've teleported into the middle of a late-night drink with them, and it wastes no time digging into various nerve endings that challenge and corroborate their ideas of realism. It's clear from the book that both Graham and Manuel are not only colleagues with affection and respect for each other's work, but that they also see themselves as realists with some degree of overlapping interests and common ground.

Manuel DeLanda

NEW YORK, NY

The specific notion of context that I want to talk about tonight is socioeconomic context. The problem here is one we inherited from social scientists. We have the micro-scale, which is the level of individual persons, and the macro-scale, which is the level of society as a whole.

Prior to the 20th century, the micro was discussed by economists in what we call microeconomics, and the macro by sociologists in macrosociology. Then came the Great Depression and John Maynard Keynes, a British economist, realized that the problems were at a scale too large to be dealt with through microeconomics. To understand this, one had to join things like overall rate of unemployment, rate of inflation, and gross national product—all of which were statistics that come out of a government dealing with an entire country. So, Keynes invented macroeconomics.

Finally, in the 1960s, a bunch of rebel sociologists invented microsociology, whether in the social constructivist school of thought, or the ethnomethodology school of thought. Rather than dealing with rational decision making, like microeconomists, they dealt with the role of routines and habits, in which there is no choice but which nevertheless shapes your daily behavior.

This is where we are today. We have sociology and economics for the micro-scale, and sociology and economics for the macro-scale. The problem is that there's an entire intermediate set of scales between those two. We can use the physicist term for this: the meso-scale, meso meaning "in between."

In the case of physicists, they need this scale in order to do experiments on entities that exist between, say, an atom of gold, which would be the micro-scale for them, and a chunk of gold, which would represent the macro-scale. Between those two, there are crystals, which grow together into grains, and ultimately reach the macro level of a piece of gold you can hold in your hand. So they invented the term meso-scale.

In the case of socioeconomics, those intermediate scales encompass most of the things that an architect would consider context. After all, for an architect to think of loadbearing structures with the functionality of a building, you cannot think just of the micro-level of the person that's going to inhabit that building or society as a whole.

Then we have an even larger scale. We have social justice movements, in which many communities may come together to extract rights from the government. Organizations can form larger entities like industrial networks or governments. The United States government is ultimately an ecosystem of many semi-autonomous organizations.

There are buildings that house those organizations, which come together to form neighborhoods. Then come the cities that are made of all those neighborhoods together with an infrastructure for transportation, and an infrastructure for water, electricity, and food. Then come the urban regions that many of those cities form. When those regions come together, they form a state. And finally, this heterogeneity of states makes up a country.

Your needs for tools to think about socioeconomic context cannot come from the micro-level or the macro-level exclusively. You need that meso-scale.

I introduced the concept of the meso-scale in my early books, and showed that each one of those intermediate levels has a history. Communities have their own history; there is a history of social justice movements; a history of industrial networks and governments; a history of cities.

There is not a single flow of time encompassing all of history the way you would believe if you believe in the macro-level of society as a whole. When you're building in a city, you'll have to interact with surrounding buildings and zoning laws that come from specific city governments. You're not dealing with society as a whole.

Philosophically, the most important concept to free the meso-scale from the tyranny of the micro and macro vision is the concept of emergent property. This concept is not new. It was introduced by chemists as early as the 1780s because they were the first scientists that practiced both chemical analysis and synthesis. They noticed very early on that water has properties such as being a solvent, but that when you break down water into hydrogen and oxygen, you lose those properties. It can be recovered if you synthesize water from that oxygen and hydrogen again.

In this way, chemists are unlike physicists, who practice mostly analysis. When you practice mostly analysis you tend to be reductionist—you analyze things all the way into atoms, then subatomic particles, then even smaller particles, and then you tend to think that everything is just a soup of subatomic particles. You will think that this meso-scale world in which we live is an illusion, and that the only reality is the smallest thing.

As architects, you practice synthesis. You understand that not every arrangement of structural elements is going to be able to deal with gravity. Only certain arrangements have the emergent capacity to bear loads, because they can transmit forces and loads all the way to the foundation in a very specific configuration. The final building cannot be reduced to its components; it has something that emerges from the specific arrangement of it.

The concept of an emergent property was first introduced into philosophy by John Stuart Mill. While he didn't yet use the word "emergence," he used water as an example of something that cannot be reduced to its component parts.

Unfortunately, then came a wave of philosophers called emergentists in the late 19th century and beginning of the 20th century. They were very enthusiastic about the idea that there was a way of blocking reductionism by thinking about novelty. If a synthesis has never occurred before, the new properties that it produces are new properties. In other words, innovation is possible.

Consider the importance of this to architects. If every design was given already, your aspirations of being the most original architect ever would be just a dream. But if innovation is possible in principle, because of emergent properties, then the world is open-ended.

Going back to socioeconomic context, we need to be able to show that each one of the levels that I mentioned—communities, organizations, cities, urban regions—have properties that are properties of the whole, but that are not in the parts.

For instance, think of a tightly knit community in which everybody knows everybody else. The connectivity of the community is a property of the social network that makes up the community, but is not a proper view of individual persons that live there. When that connectivity reaches a certain degree of density, gossip or hearsay will travel very quickly throughout the community, particularly if a piece of gossip is about anything that breaks a local norm.

In other words, the community as a whole can store reputations; what other people think about you, which depends on your history in the community. When that reputation reaches a certain threshold of damage, then the local community can also enforce those local norms via ridicule or ostracism.

When someone is laughing behind your back, the reason it hurts is that they are members of the community. So, the ability to enforce local norms is not a property that's reducible to persons, but a property of the community.

A similar thing happens with organizations—they have an authority structure. Doctors give commands to nurses, who give commands to patients. The warden of a prison gives commands to the guards, who give commands to the prisoners. The people that belong to that organization need to believe that the authority is legitimate, that those people can give orders because of their position in the hierarchy. But legitimacy cannot be reduced to the beliefs of the individual persons that make up the organization; the legitimacy is an emergent property of an entire organization.

The idea here is that we need to bridge the micro and the macro. We have several layers, but each layer needs to specify not only what emergent properties and capacities it has, but how they come about. The modern concept of emerging properties is not just that it is a property of a whole that's not in the parts, but it has a second component that says that it is a property that is caused by specific interactions between the parts.

Social justice movements as a whole are made out of many communities. There's not a single social justice movement in history—not the worker's movement, the civil rights movement, or the women's movement—that was done by a single community. You cannot extract rights from the government with a single community demonstrating in front of a government building. You need to display numerousness and solidarity amongst a group of communities.

If the different members of that coalition now begin fighting with each other, that property of solidarity at the level of the whole movement disappears, because you need those interactions for the properties to exist.

The concept of emerging property has now been validated, has been freed from the mysticism of the original philosophers who thought about it, and is a very reputable concept. It is the concept that we need not only to think, "how do load-bearing properties emerge in a load-bearing structure?" But we need it to be able to think about the full complexity and historicity of the massive scale.

Graham Harman

LOS ANGELES, CA

Since Manuel talked about emergence and the meso-level, I want to start with the equivalent of those ideas in my own philosophy. I use the terms *overmining* and *undermining* to discuss the problems of philosophy.

Undermining simply means you're reducing things downward, analyzing them into their tiniest pieces, such as often done in physics. In philosophy, this was the dominant method in the so-called pre-Socratic period around 600-500 BCE. Rather than philosophers, I would call these thinkers "speculative physicists" because they say everything's made of air, earth, fire, and water; joined by love and separated by hate. There has to be a formless *Apeiron*, a blob-like continuum that things emerge from and pass back into. As Manuel described, the problem with this kind of philosophy is that it destroys all the mid-level objects. You can't talk about emergence if you're reducing everything to its tiniest pieces. In the modern period, there tends to be the opposite approach of going upward.

Overmining means that instead of saying that objects are too shallow to be real and that you should go beneath the surface, you are saying they're too deep to be real and we should therefore look only at the top. Undermining and overmining usually go together because the weaknesses of each approach needs the other to defend its weaknesses. A lot of philosophies are simply ways of trying to get rid of that intermediate level and reduce things either to the bottommost or topmost layers of the cosmos. The term I came up with for this was duomining, which means you get the two different types of reduction simultaneously.

Aristotle wrote a lot of important books, from those on ethics to those on aesthetics and poetics. But two of his primary books are the *Physics* and the *Metaphysics*. *Physics* talks about nature, while *Metaphysics* talks about philosophical matters that are other than or above nature in some way. Similarly, *Physics* was about the continuous and *Metaphysics* was about the discreet.

You can find the continuous and discrete everywhere in intellectual history. In evolutionary theory, for example, the Darwinists typically talk about gradual evolution from big fish eating little fish and reproducing bigger baby fish. Over time the fish get bigger or more ferocious. Paleontologists Stephen Jay Gould and Niles Eldredge talked about punctuated equilibria, where evolution occurs in jumps. Evolutionary theorist Lynn Margulis spoke of serial endosymbiosis, where evolution only happens through the joining together of two previous separate life forms.

Continua are things that cannot be separated into parts except potentially through the work of your mind. My presentation this evening is 20 minutes, so you could say that there are 20 separate instants of time in my lecture, but you could also divide it up into 1,200 seconds or 2,400 half-seconds. Or maybe you want to divide it up thematically so that if I have four major points I'm trying to make, there are four parts to my presentation.

Aristotle would say that there is no definite number of time units in this presentation; you can divide it up any way you want. But for Aristotle, there is one thing that you cannot just divide up any way you please. How many people are in this room? There is a definite number of people in this room, because we're not bleeding into one giant human. We are not a continuum. We relate to each other in some ways, while also closing off from each other in other ways. Aristotle calls such definite things substances; I call them objects.

What I do not like about Aristotle's concept of substances is that he tends to focus on natural ones, like plants and animals. What about things like aircrafts or regional metropolises the size of Pittsburgh or Buffalo? I would consider them to be objects. An object for me is not a hard, physical solid that endures over time. There are some things that last very brief moments that I would still consider an object. An object for me is something that cannot be reduced in either direction; it cannot be undermined or overmined.

It's something that is resistant; it's emergence beyond its pieces. It is perhaps also submergent; beneath its current environments. It is something that is not fully identifiable with what it's made of or what it does.

If somebody asks you what something is, they're asking you a knowledge question. There are only two kinds of answers you can give: you can explain what something is made of or what it does. But by answering in this way, you are either reducing something downward or reducing it upward. This puts Triple O in the position of needing to talk about a kind of cognition that is not the same as knowledge. This is why I favor the kind of cognition that we see in the arts and, in my opinion, also in philosophy.

You can analyze Picasso's *Guernica* (1937) as made up of 40 percent canvas, 50 percent pigment, and 10 percent something else, but that doesn't tell you anything about the painting. It's also not good art criticism if you only tell the story of the Spanish Civil War that led Picasso to paint this work. If this is a good painting, it should be of aesthetic interest 2,000 years from now, when people have forgotten the details of the Spanish Civil War. It has to go beyond its context.

In this way, I have sympathies with formalism. This is opposed to people who want to politicize the arts and architecture; who make it purely contextual or ecological. Art and architecture is somehow cut off from its context in both directions. It is not made of its beams, but it's also not completely reducible to the effect it has on its current context.

To further explain my use of the term formalism: when I say form, I'm talking about something the Medievals used to call "substantial form," which means the reality of a thing that is never perfectly manifest. It's the nature of a thing here and now, and this doesn't need to be eternal.

Kant only used the term formalism in connection with his ethics, which famously outline that an ethical act is not to be determined by its consequences, nor by its motives. An ethical act is to be done purely out of a sense of duty. If in a police state they ask if someone's hiding in your attic, you're not supposed to lie, according to Kant. If you did lie, you would not be following the universal obligation of evolved rational beings to tell the truth and you are thereby undercutting everyone's commitment to truth; you're undermining the entire system on which truth is based. This is what we call formalism in ethics.

Kant also had an idea of objective beauty that everyone should agree on. It's not about the objects, it's about the transcendental structure of human cognition that causes us all to respond to beautiful works in the same way. The visual art critics of the 20th century who were most responsive to Kant's philosophy flipped that around. They didn't want it to be about us, but about the art object. For example, Michael Fried does not want artworks that rely on theatrics or play on our emotions.

That reversal aside, they still agree that formalism, which is supposed to be about one thing being cut off from another, must be a separation specifically between human consciousness and the world. Those are the two basic zones of reality for all modern philosophy—you have the thinking subject and the rest of the world with all its many different types of objects.

It seems to me that this is impossible. You can't have non-theatrical arts or architecture, because there is no way to have an aesthetic experience without deep human involvement. Look at a metaphor like Homer's "wine dark sea" in *The Odyssey*; it does not just literally mean that the wine and the sea are of approximately the same color. What makes it a metaphorical statement is that the literal comparison between the wine and the sea is simply a pretext for us to bring a lot of the sea's other qualities onto the wine or vice versa. The sea is not just getting the color of the wine, but also the drunkenness and the oblivion that we associate with wine.

This is very different from literal language, in which you are equating an object with a set of properties that you think belong to it. There's no distinction between the object and its qualities. If you say a pen is like a pencil, you are showing that two objects have roughly the same properties—they can both write, they're long and skinny, and fairly cheap.

With a literal statement you can always reverse the two terms and it doesn't matter the order in which you say them. That is not true of aesthetic statements. You cannot say, "wine dark sea" and "sea dark wine" and mean the same.

There is also no way to paraphrase that metaphor or to put it in literal language. The object is somehow elusive. There cannot be qualities floating in space without an object; qualities are always inflected by the object to which they belong. The object sea has vanished from beyond our view in the case of the wine dark sea and we ourselves must step in its place. Therefore, we become the real object that is embodying these "wine dark sea" qualities. And this is why metaphor always has a theatrical component.

So, what I'm really against is literalism. You can never give an exhaustive prose description that's definitive about any painting or building. You lose something when you overmine or undermine such work.

Kant talks about beauty just like ethics, as something that cannot be contaminated with any ulterior principle, such as utility. An ethical act is not ethical because it's useful. Kant also thinks an artwork is not beautiful just because it happens to please. This is why he has such a low estimation of architecture. It can never rise to the level of pure beauty because it's contaminated with utility.

Now, I've tried to suggest that beauty is always already contaminated with the human element because it has to be theatrical. Therefore, I think Kant's point about that is moot. Nonetheless, there is still a question of how we get non-literal and non-relational utility. This would be the job of architecture.

Conversation

MANUEL DELANDA AND GRAHAM HARMAN MODERATED BY FERDA KOLATAN

Ferda Kolatan: Graham and Manuel's writing has been very important to me as an architect. Manuel's thinking has been influential to the field since the early 1990s. It coincided with the advent of generative software tools in the field of design, providing an intellectual framework for the early days of digital design experimentation. Many digital pioneers found overlaps and converging interests in Manuel's materialism. It is easy to grasp why his work on material systems—his unique take on history, emergence, and singularities—became hotly debated items in design studios, panels, and conferences.

Manuel's influence and relevance to our field, of course, is not limited to the early days of the digital. Like the digital project itself, it has evolved and bifurcated into many strands. But I believe it's important to locate the time and circumstances of the shift from postmodern and the deconstructivist discourses in architecture toward a generative materialist position and the role Manuel's writing played in this.

Graham's work appeared on the architect's radar about a decade and a half after the advent of generative digital design, at a time when the digital had proliferated into many directions. This variety of interest and the maturation of the digital project softened the more coherent discursive focus of the earlier experimental phases. In this context, Speculative Realism—Triple O in particular—provided a new lens through which to reexamine the digital discourse. In fact, the architects who initially became interested in Triple O were almost exclusively from the first digitally trained student generation coming out of the 1990s. Moreover, these were the architects who had branched into the group investigating the aesthetic effects of digital design. This shift away from questions regarding generative processes and toward the subject of sensation was one of the reasons Graham's work resonated so well.

When I was reading through the discussion you published in the book *The Rise of Realism*, I was struck by your conversation about what identifies the object or what you would determine as the real. I think Manuel talks about history and maintenance, which is pointing toward a larger context within which the identity of an object is being determined. In contrast to that, Graham believes it's an essence that makes the identity of an object. I find it interesting to understand how both of those lend themselves to be understood as ontologies that generate or account for change and novelty. Can you both elaborate on this a bit more?

Manuel DeLanda: Let me first point out some places where our two approaches overlap or coincide. The word "object" in Graham's terminology is similar to what I call an "individual entity." The problem here is that the word "individual" has become synonymous with "person." Now "individual person" sounds redundant, but that is just an accident of linguistic history. The word "individual" simply means that something is unique, non-repeatable.

In addition to that, Graham and I share the idea that we should not place a human characteristic, like our capacity to know something, as our criteria for something being real. Between the idea that there is nothing in the world that consciousness did not already put in it and the idea that the world exists entirely independent of our consciousness, there's an intermediate position called "empiricism." It says that things that are directly visible are mind-independent, but things that are not directly perceivable are just theoretical concepts or constructs.

While I say that the world exists entirely independent of our minds, clearly cities are not entirely independent of our minds because if we all died, if our minds disappeared, cities would stop functioning. Communities, organizations, social justice movements, governments, countries would also stop working. They stop being what they are if our minds disappeared. So, in the case of social entities, we need to say they are independent of the contents of our minds, which is another point of agreement between Graham and me.

Where we seem to differ is in the role of history. For me, having a birth and having a death is what defines you as an individual. The human species is not an eternal thing, like Aristotle used to think. It came into existence at a particular moment, when we became reproductively isolated from chimpanzees and other primates or from their ancestors, and it could die if we go extinct.

I can perfectly agree with Graham that there are limits to what we can know about these entities. In his own version of philosophy, he wants to make this something that withdraws from our knowledge and what gives identities to things. Whereas for me, identity is something that emerges from your life experience, from your psychological and physical scars, from your memories of past events.

Lastly, we both share the idea that individual entities or objects are what used to be called in medieval times *haecceities*. It is the "thisness" of something; when you cannot characterize something by any other way than by pointing at it and saying "this." Graham characterizes that in terms of what he call "singular essences." I have problems with essences, but for him, essences are always singular and therefore they are haecceities. For me, they are very close to what I call historicity of individuals.

Graham Harman: I would agree with all of this as an assessment of our agreements and disagreements. I'll just add a couple of things. I see the history of an entity as being important, but not globally important. Most of an entity's history is forgotten because it's irrelevant. There are only a few stages in a thing's history that are inscribed in the heart of a thing. If you think about your own life, what are the moments that are most important? Almost never are they moments when you were sitting around in your bedroom, brooding about how to find yourself. There's a finite number of such important moments in your life. Once you reach a certain stage of maturity, nothing changes you the way that earlier experiences tend to do.

I know Manuel doesn't like the word "essence" as much as I do, although it turns out it's hardly a terminological difference. To me, essence simply means that a thing is what it is and you can't make it what it's not. It's part of the essence of water to be a solvent. But what you find in the critique of essence from people like Edward Said and Judith Butler, is something different, which is harmful. They're talking about the knowledge of essence. In *Orientalism* (1978), Edward Said is talking about

From left to right: David Erdman, Graham Harman, Manuel DeLanda, and Ferda Kolatan in conversation at Pratt Sessions 12.

the domination of the Orient by western powers, which makes a lot of sense. But then he says things like, "There is no essence of Egypt. There's just individual Egyptians," there's a problem there.

When I moved to Egypt, I had to read up a bit on Egyptian culture. There are certain things you don't do there that you can do here and vice versa. Of course, there is going to be individual variation, but on the whole, there is some sense in talking about an Egyptian society apart from the individuals, or even different zones of Egypt having their own cultures.

The part where essentialism becomes harmful is when people claim to know it. My favorite examples of this is to look at the Scandinavians, who are considered now to be the most civil people in Europe with these wonderful welfare states and gender equality. But go back a thousand years and they were Vikings raping nuns and burning libraries. So, what's the essence of the Scandinavians? Essence is something that is deeper than its manifestations.

Kolatan: I want to come back to this point of novelty or emergence. Graham, it seems to me that it's non-negotiable that you need the withdrawn object in order to draw from what you call the "hidden surplus." To you, this the foundation of change and emergence, and therefore novelty. Would that be a correct assessment? If so, that's radically different from Manuel's perspective. It is a difference that associates the context—spatial as well as temporal—as the engine of production. This difference has a lot of ramifications.

Harman: Since Manuel's background is in Deleuze, I suspect the default state for him is more a dynamic nature of reality. For me, the default state of reality is an inert state where objects are what they are, unless some outside force forms a relationship with them and causes them to change.

Manuel and I are both realists. I loved his first email response to me ever, which was that he was glad to meet a fellow realist like me because, for decades, calling oneself a realist was like calling oneself a child molester in philosophy. Realism was so unpopular. But Manuel likes "materialism" as a term along with realism, whereas I'm not as fond of materialism. It's partly because I think everything has a form and the term materialism can sometimes open the doors to a certain overly mathematized vision of reality. I'm thinking here of Quentin Meillassoux, my former colleague in Speculative Realism.

Meillassoux thinks that you can know the primary qualities of things mathematically. It seems to me that he has a big philosophical problem then because there's something in the form of the real dog that is not captured in the mathematical model. Meillassoux simply thinks the mathematical model of a dog is stamped into "dead matter," as he calls it. But we don't know what this dead matter is. We've never seen it. It's a theoretical posit that, somewhere out there, there's matter.

DeLanda: There are many traditions of materialist philosophy. The most famous one, which I completely reject, is dialectical materialism, which says that the negation of the negation, thesis and antithesis, is the way of generating a form in the world. Historical materialism is based on misconceptions about economic history. And when an analytical philosopher calls himself or herself a materialist, they are typically reductionist. Those kinds of materialisms are dogmatic, because they are not based on evidence.

I simply added the word "neo" to my materialism to say this is a new type of materialism. When we take matter and we inject it with energy to push it away from equilibrium, it begins doing things that we didn't know it could do. It begins self-organizing, an idea that is very closely related to the concept of emerging property, but it has different connotations. Self-organizing is what allows a new type of materialism, which believes that matter is active and has its own morphogenetic capacities.

Kolatan: I would like to shift focus to potentialities. It seems you have slightly different takes on this as well.

Harman: I'm not sure whether this is just a difference of terminology or difference of thought. We both see the problems with potential. To go back, Aristotle invents the concept of potentiality when he's talking about the metaphysics of his rivals, the Megarians from Megara in Athens, who thought that nobody is anything other than what they're actually doing right now. You would not be a house builder unless you're building this very second. So, what's the difference between me and a master house builder that's sleeping? There's obviously a big difference, even though neither of us is building right now. In response to this, Artistotle invents the concept of potentiality. The only problem I have with that is that it treats the reality of a thing too much in relation to the other thing. Artistotle would call us a "capacity." I think there are things within a thing that aren't expressed, that are not necessarily capacities, but are somehow intrinsic to the thing itself.

DeLanda: We talked about this in the book. To make this very clear: if you have a knife in your hand right now that knife has certain properties that are both real, independently of our minds, and actual. The knife weighs a certain amount, has a certain length and a sheen at this moment. But it also has capacities, which is that the knife has the capacity to cut things. Right now, it's not cutting anything, but that doesn't mean that it could not be cutting something.

Capacities are different in that they are real and mind-independent, but they are not necessarily actual. Another important thing about capacities is a point emphasized by Deleuze: the capacity of the knife to cut can only be exercised with something that has the capacity to be cut, or the capacity to be affected. Cheese, bread, and lettuce have the capacity to be cut, but a solid block of titanium does not have the capacity to be cut by a knife. It has the capacity to be cut by a laser, but then that's a different tool altogether.

Capacities are open-ended. How do you limit those capacities? After all, that knife could have all kinds of bizarre capacities that we don't even understand. Is there an infinite number of capacities? If so, how do we think about that infinity?

Here, I need to introduce the concept of the space of possibilities. This concept is much clearer when we talk about tendencies, which are similar to capacities. We know that a gallon of liquid water will become ice, if we lower the temperature to zero degrees Celsius. If we increase the temperature to 100 degrees, it will become vapor. Right now, the water is liquid, so being ice and vapor exists only potentially.

The space of possibilities for water, as it responds to temperature, has been structured by the singularities of the boiling point and the freezing point. In a diagram, with just this one parameter of temperature, these two appear as critical points. If you add a second parameters, pressure, they appear as critical lines. If you add a third dimension, volume, now they appear as surfaces.

We don't have a similar way of defining capacities. How do we discuss all the ways that knives can interact: to cut, to murder, to kill? This is what Graham rightly defines as a problem; there's a hole in the theory. If you don't have a principal way of enumerating the possibilities, all kinds of possibilities become available to you. So, we need a more rigorous way of thinking about the structure of possibility spaces, because that is also what gives us the sense of novelty.

The space of possible architectural designs is not a closed space. By adding new stylistic nuances and new stylistic strategies, architects add dimensions to the space. A great architect can make a very dramatic interruption, changing architectural history by showing that you can do things differently. We don't have the tools yet to pinpoint the dramatic moments in the history of our city and community, in the history of an organization. And so, I accept the complaint that I come up short there. My theory only works for tendencies, which are the simplest one of potentialities. I'm hopeful that I can expand that and that the future generation will expand it even more. It will finally give us a sense of potentiality that is not vague and nebulous.

Audience Question: How do we make use of these ideas? What does architecture do with this? There are projects that are allegedly products of these ideas: we see forms trying to defy the materials of which they're made, and we see architects trying to evade preconceptions. But I haven't seen the evidence that you need this heavy operating system of Speculative Realism or Triple O to understand these works.

Harman: One of my principles, since getting involved in the architectural world, is that it's not my job to legislate anything. As architects, you work with different materials and problems than we do. So, it's a question of trying to do my best work and hoping I stimulate students and others around me to follow that. On the other hand, it's also fait accompli, because you've just gone through decades of philosophers having an immense impact on the discipline. There's a pushback against that now, but you had phenomenological architecture coming out of Heidegger, you had deconstructivism in Derrida, and then you had a Deleuzian wave. Sometimes there's resentment from architects, who think that philosophers are trying to tell them what to do. This is certainly not what I'm trying to do. Hopefully we can be an interesting stimulant for architects to take, like pills; it shows them new visions.

Kolatan: None of these ideas are ever meant to be used like a formula to produce architecture. I know some people do that, but I think those people are largely misguided. But it is important to understand architecture as a profession of cultural production. And this cultural production does not come from a singular place; it engages with other modes of cultural production. Architecture is a unique profession in the sense that we have to understand culture in a larger context.

Overview

Pratt GAUD
PASQUARELLI
SHoP ARCHITECTS
NEW YORK
02.15.18
THURSDAY 6PM
HIGGINS HALL AUDITORIUM
POP UP EXHIBITION
PRATT SESSIONS 07

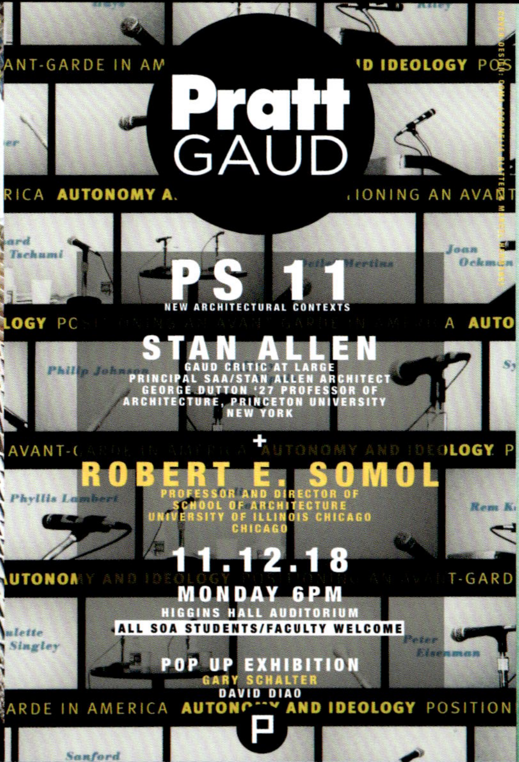
Pratt GAUD
PS 11
NEW ARCHITECTURAL CONTEXTS
STAN ALLEN
GAUD CRITIC AT LARGE
PRINCIPAL SAA/STAN ALLEN ARCHITECT
GEORGE DUTTON '27 PROFESSOR OF
ARCHITECTURE, PRINCETON UNIVERSITY
NEW YORK
+
ROBERT E. SOMOL
PROFESSOR AND DIRECTOR OF
SCHOOL OF ARCHITECTURE
UNIVERSITY OF ILLINOIS CHICAGO
CHICAGO
11.12.18
MONDAY 6PM
HIGGINS HALL AUDITORIUM
ALL SOA STUDENTS/FACULTY WELCOME
POP UP EXHIBITION
GARY SCHALTER
DAVID DIAO

Pratt GAUD
PS12
PRATT SESSIONS TWELVE
NEW ARCHITECTURAL CONTEXT
MANUEL DE LANDA
PHILOSOPHER
PRATT GAUD ADJUNCT PROFESSOR
NEW YORK
+
GRAHAM HARMAN
PHILOSOPHER
DISTINGUISHED PROFESSOR OF PHILOSOPHY,SCI-ARC
LOS ANGELES
FERDA KOLATAN
MODERATOR
11.15.18
THURSDAY 6PM
HIGGINS HALL AUDITORIUM
ALL SOA STUDENTS/FACULTY WELCOME
PRATT SESSIONS VOL.1 BOOK LAUNCH
POP UP EXHIBITION
LEE BONTECOU
MIA FEUER

C4

Pratt
GAUD
PS07
MALTZAN
MICHAEL MALTZAN ARCHITECTURE
LOS ANGELES
+
PASQUARELLI
SHoP ARCHITECTS
NEW YORK
02.15.18
THURSDAY 6PM
HIGGINS HALL AUDITORIUM
POP UP EXHIBITION
PRATT SESSIONS 07
NEW ARCHITECTURAL CONTEXTS

PHOTO CREDIT: SAA/STAN ALLEN ARCHITECT
Pratt
GAUD
PS 11
NEW ARCHITECTURAL CONTEXTS
STAN ALLEN
GAUD CRITIC AT LARGE
PRINCIPAL SAA/STAN ALLEN ARCHITECT
GEORGE DUTTON '27 PROFESSOR OF
ARCHITECTURE, PRINCETON UNIVERSITY
NEW YORK
+
ROBERT E. SOMOL
PROFESSOR AND DIRECTOR OF
SCHOOL OF ARCHITECTURE
UNIVERSITY OF ILLINOIS CHICAGO
CHICAGO
11.12.18
MONDAY 6PM
HIGGINS HALL AUDITORIUM
ALL SOA STUDENTS/FACULTY WELCOME
POP UP EXHIBITION
GARY SCHALTER
DAVID DIAO
P

COVER DESING: BRUCE MAU DESIGN INC.
Pratt
GAUD
PS 12
PRATT SESSIONS TWELVE
NEW ARCHITECTURAL CONTEXT
MANUEL DE LANDA
PHILOSOPHER
PRATT GAUD ADJUNCT PROFESSOR
NEW YORK
+
GRAHAM HARMAN
PHILOSOPHER
DISTINGUISHED PROFESSOR OF PHILOSOPHY,SCI-ARC
LOS ANGELES
FERDA KOLATAN
MODERATOR
11.15.18
THURSDAY 6PM
HIGGINS HALL AUDITORIUM
ALL SOA STUDENTS/FACULTY WELCOME
PRATT SESSIONS VOL.1 BOOK LAUNCH
POP UP EXHIBITION
LEE BONTECOU
MIA FEUER
SWERVE
P

CONTEXTS

Vol. 2

MEDIUMS

Pratt Sessions

Mediums

David Erdman
New Architectural Mediums

In *Pratt Sessions*, half of our talks will introduce the subject of New Architectural Mediums. We are intentionally conflating medium and media. The purpose of such a focus is to intensify a number of standing debates and to stimulate nerve endings within the discipline and profession that we (at the GAUD) feel are important and will remain important in the coming decades; an issue that is (in retrospect to these sessions) underscored by the pandemic moment in which we are situated. In short, it is an effort to unleash the limits of the (now) somewhat traditional software-based representational media that enable architectural drawing, modeling, and prototyping as well as unleash the temporal processes (mediums) found in buildings (artificial/natural light, horticulture, screens and graphics, among others) as a means to investigate their potentials from an explicitly post-digital, post-geometrical, post-human vantage point. We aim to examine the extent to which we could understand them as highly synthetic, design-driven components of our architectural and urban environments, and to move them into the realm of live experience. Each of the Pratt Sessions participants offers a vantage point on the subjects of architectural media/mediums, and each pairing raises specific questions surrounding the prospect of those subjects: namely what is an "architectural" media and/or medium and why would either be valuable now or in the future?

From the aesthetics of color and live rendering to the alive, post-human, and supercharged ways in which we interact with design mediums, to differing methodologies of codified and built drawing, the three Pratt Sessions collected here and the diverse array of participants from both coasts definitively trace an emerging and important discourse. Supported by invigorated track records of built work and/or writing to underpin their claims and the points being made by our coveted participants, the discussions and presentations encapsulated here present concise snippets, glimpses of how our understanding of media might change as a discipline and profession. It is equally important to note that each practice, participant, designer, and thinker operates within a multitude of media and mediums, bringing them together primarily through the contemporary experience of the human subject in relation to the architectural environments they study or design. Finally, it is worth noting that each speaker diminishes the idea that there is any such thing as singular "essential" architectural media or medium (as has been historically espoused via innumerable architectural treatises on space, light, and movement), while also implicitly insisting upon the idea that one would only arrive at a particular experience, or at a specific configuration/combination of media through architectural design.

The framing for the discussions is meant to be provocative, theoretical, and historical. The association of architecture and media may seem odd. Media is ephemeral—that which is not permanent—it's fleeting. Mediums are equally intangible, slippery. Whether one considers pop cultural media, branding, graphics, signage, or mediums like light, air, or water, none would be associated with the conventional cultural assumptions about architecture, its permanence, its object orientation, or its weight. Media and mediums are the stuff architecture contains as opposed to the "skin and bones" of Architecture proper with a capital "A." Importantly, these disassociations between architecture, media, and mediums further reinforce contemporary and historical propensities toward architectures of purity, autonomy, and away from everything capital and commercial for which the fluidity and expendable qualities of media stand. In short, the following sessions examine, perturb, and irritate the idea that media and mediums are the things that one might consider "outside" of architecture and opportunistically include them as a necessary tool kit for architects, our entrepreneurial thinking, our innovation, and the expansion of our practice and discourse.

These three sessions also recognize that both media and mediums have always been enmeshed in architecture; though perhaps simply not historicized or canonized as such, which might be another way of saying architecture has an ephemeral, superficial, and fleeting yet parallel counterpart. Drawing upon quantum theory, one could understand this parallelism as the simultaneous co-existing and enmeshing of alternative realities through architecture and its live experiences; more specifically through its potential and perceived dimensionalities or inter-dimensional capacity. Underscoring this concept of highly

mediated interdimensional architecture are two buildings from antiquity that are perhaps radically misunderstood and/or under-explored for their potential; the Pantheon and the Parthenon. Each separately introduces medium and media as necessary parts of architecture: the Pantheon—a building designed around a medium, one window shaping light—and the Parthenon—a vessel-container for many narrative and pop cultural stories (communicative media), including its war story frieze and caryatids etched, sculpted, and painted into the building.

An important commonality among these two examples touches upon their illusive aspects and the fact that they tinker with dimensionality. Elements—architectural and otherwise—shift between 2D, 3D, and 4D. There is an entanglement of media; here again borrowing from the lexicon of quantum theory and the notion of "entangled" electrons that form parallel universes. In each of these canons of history architecture, sculpture, drawing, graphics, painting, air, and/or light vibrate in and out of focus, shift scales, alter perceived depths and densities of content or information, allowing one to experience a rich texture of live and virtual spaces, simultaneously evoking what today might be called an "intermedia" experience. As exhaustively studied as these two buildings are, it is uncommon to recognize their mediatric capacities and how they introduce the ways in which buildings can convert specific media "technologies" and mediums (often from other disciplines, other professions or literally from "outside") and galvanize them into live architectural experiences. They each embrace contamination and use other media and mediums as fodder, making them a reciprocal and inextricable agent in the architecture; they are not "contained" but activated and activating the subjects immersed within them.

While the history of this is fascinating, ripe for exploration, and implicit in these sessions, a subject of greater interest at the GAUD is the value of understanding the use of media and mediums at the turn of the 21st century—is it valuable or not? From the digital to the post-digital, the Pratt Sessions speculate that it may be worth extending our understanding of media beyond the representational and the generative; beyond modeling, drawing, prototyping software and to engage in alternative emerging forms of live communication. This opens the door to explore the intersection of where the representational becomes experiential or conceived in real-time. Each of the participants as individuals, firms and in their pairings are curated to create hinge points of this discourse—expanding it and reinscribing both its futures and its histories.

Circling back to the above-noted point and in a broader context, it is perfectly reasonable to wonder why this examination of media and mediums might be important to a graduate school of architecture today or for the future of its students. In short, we hope to demystify the many media and mediums available to students—from software and robots to green walls and energy production—and give them a framework for understanding how to engage them as architects and within the realm of their design work. This strain of the Pratt Sessions thus lauds new concepts of architectural media. It sees this discourse and debate as necessary for a contemporary graduate student's education and sees the subject as bona fide theoretical, conceptual, and design substance key to their education and the profession into which they will enter; and hopefully alter. This second trio of Pratt Sessions on Architectural Media and Mediums evolves our interpretations and concepts of how and why mediums continue to be important in our curriculum and thinking as a department. They are a foundation that welcomes a broader understanding of these concepts with the hope that they will offer our students and the GAUD community an opportunity to use technology in deep and meaningful ways that enable them to engage extra-disciplinary audiences and expand architecture thinking, its role in leadership and its potential praxes.

Pita & Bloom

Young &
Ayata

01

03

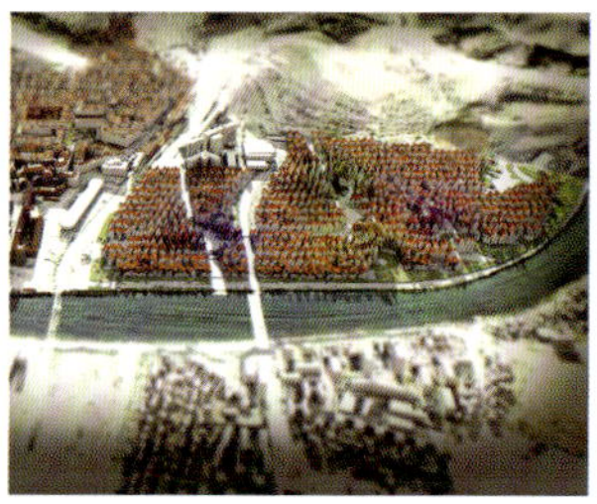

04

07

02

05

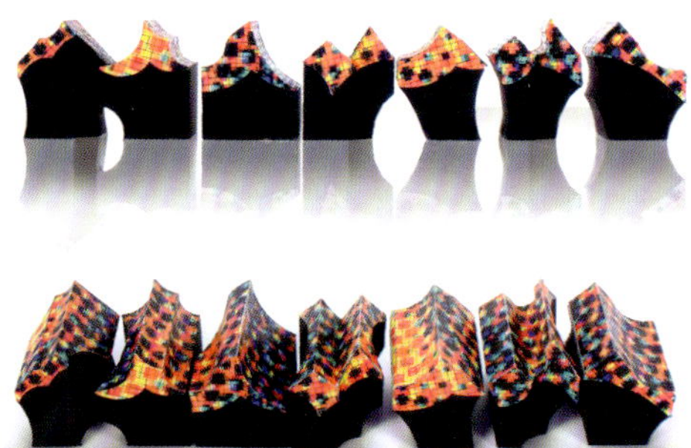

06

08

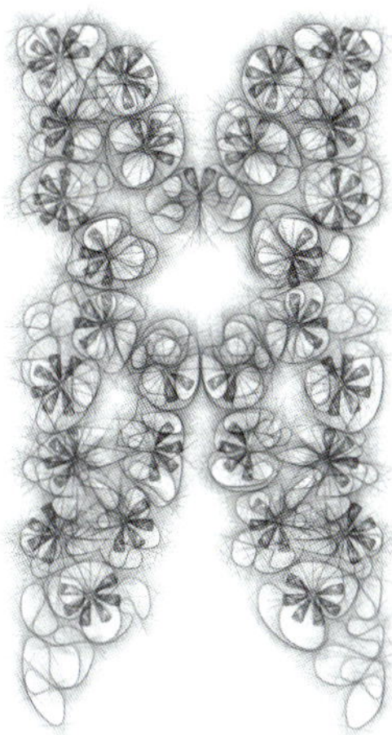

10

12

15

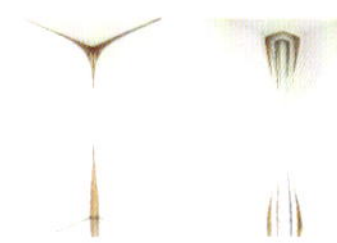

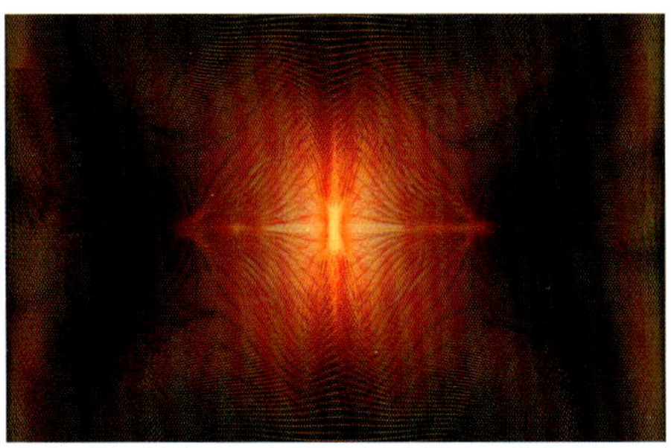

09

11

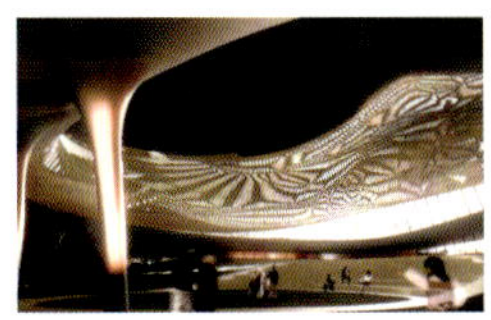

13

14

Introduction

DAVID ERDMAN

It's my pleasure to introduce our four guests this evening: Florencia Pita and Jackilin Hah Bloom, and Michael Young and Kutan Ayata. They all test the limits of media and what it means to practice architecture, stretching it into a territory that goes beyond mere building. They each use digital media and fabrication technologies in extensive ways, *and* there is a lot of color that you'll notice moving around.

There are two key distinguishing characteristics that I can draw out in Pita and Bloom's work in relation to media. The first is that their work is unabashedly about the surface and an embrace of the "supergraphic." **01** The thinness of the surface contrasts against its thickness; it ranges from veneer to poche. They play in a territory between the "Superflat" and extreme bas-relief. **02** Graphic techniques intricately combine and layer hatching, tone, and dot-matrices to produce an implicit depth in what is otherwise flat. These visual arrays are unleashed across landscapes or villages. **03**

Scale is perverse in the work of Pita and Bloom. Moves that are deployed at the scale of design objects **04** or furniture are also engrained in large-scale architectural propositions. **05** One's ability to distinguish between a model, a prototype, or an interior environment becomes somewhat blurred; reflected also in the way they install their work in their self-designed exhibitions. This ambiguity of scale and their graphic use of coloration produces an enchanting quality not so easily achieves; a quality that comes from a highly skilled and sophisticated way of working between architectural and graphic mediums. **06** The work is *unbelievable*; it has a sense of being *unreal*. It looks imaginary and lies in a productive yet unusual territory for architecture discourse: somewhere between *The Smurfs* and *The Teletubbies*. **07**

Young and Ayata's work feels like a spirograph gone wild. **08** While their representations are developed digitally, their scripted stroke resembles various mediums: neither pencil stroke, nor ink line, nor paintbrush; stroke, line, and surface all hover somewhere in between. The effect of their drawings distorts our assumptions about the representational aspects of the media they use. **09** Similar and yet different from impressionism, drawings are built up of an incredibly dense array of lines that approximate tonal or luminous fields; they appear both digitally generated and handmade.

These drawings are in many ways abstractions of their building projects. You see the drawings enmeshed, embossed, and contoured all over the objects and building masses that they're configuring and composing. **11** The material qualities of these built drawings produce a range of patinas; some lean toward incrustation, others are more akin to water stains. **10** The patterning of the tile or color itinerary might align with the massing or disrupt it. This misalignment/alignment, slippage/conformance invokes a tense, uncomfortable quality that gives the projects a vibratory and preternatural sensibility.

Another distinguishing factor in the work of Young and Ayata is a strong sense of architectural interiority. A recurrent artifact are areas of intense color and linework that produce kaleidoscopic, often duplicated, somewhat blurry interior environments. However, these splendorous caverns are rarely revealed on the exterior. You have to burrow across the site or up into the building to get subtle glimpses. **12** You see this design obfuscation repeated as a theme throughout the projects; a palpable mysteriousness, an effect of double vision, invoking a sense of discovery. **13**

Whether it's through panelization or horticulture, they also frequently imbue that stroke with temporal effects, which seems to enrich the duration of their architecture, which juxtapose or intertwine interiority and exteriority. **14**

If Pita and Bloom are into a productive superficiality and thinness, then we might perhaps see Young and Ayata as being their counterpart, a firm whose work is about thickness and depth, deploying a continuous revealing. **15**

If one presumes that either firm is operating on the margins of mainstream architecture, I think it's somewhat intentional. Operating on the fringe is certainly among the territories available for contemporary design firms. And while we might all admire the extent to which each firm pushes the boundary of what architecture is or could be today, the work remains explicitly architectural—even if media-saturated, drenched in color, or engaged in other disciplines.

These four practitioners engage a long history of architects working with mediums that are not borne out of architecture, which range from graphic design to the brush stroke. That legacy of work continues fervently across contemporary architectural projects, and you can see it working its way across

urban territories. What is different about doing this today? What's different about the approach of four architects whose education and training are anchored in the digital turn? This is something to consider for the discussion ahead.

Florencia Pita & Jackilin Hah Bloom

LOS ANGELES, CA

We embrace design very much, and we work a lot with the medium of the drawing, the medium of the model, and the medium of representation in general.

We wanted to present our projects through color, form, and curves. The way that we take on color has to do with how color has evolved. We are interested in the progression from paint toward print and find that those stages all exist in some way in our projects. Consider the work of Joseph Albers, and the reinvention of color combinations through works like *Homage to the Square*, and then the evolution toward print media with artists like Andy Warhol. You see an evolution of print media to computer media, onto screen resolution from CMYK and RGB. It

Florencia Pita and Jackilin Hah Bloom, The New Zocalo, 15th Venice Architecture Biennale, 2018

brought colors that were nonexistent in the previous iteration.

We did a proposition for the American Pavilion at the Venice Architecture Biennale in 2018. It was a project for an elevated platform in Detroit and the focus was to engage in how color can create a surface in the public realm. We tried to evolve the idea of publicness or the idea of landscape, and bring it to the site, which was in an area called Mexicantown.

Our drawings for the project relate to an evolution of a highly-articulated landscape, such as Versailles, onto more contemporary color palettes. The blurring of the patterns and the articulations of the French garden becomes a new space for the public realm. We were also interested in the idea of layers and decay. In a city like Detroit, you see decaying buildings with many layers of peeled paint. The multi-coloration becomes a thickness.

In this way, we are interested in how flatness, color, paint, and printed images can advance or give a completely new material quality. We did a project called Flat Pools for the LA River. The name refers to the painting of pools done by David Hockney. We looked at painting the channel of the LA River, which is a flat infrastructural machine. The flatness of the pool hovers between the curves of the channel and the image could have an added effect of depth. The project has a certain literality in regards to how the flat pool operates as a kind of landscape.

We did a housing proposal for Maribor in Slovenia. The idea was that the image of the landscape of the context of Maribor, which is surrounded by mountains, would have been converted into a halftone pattern overlaid on to the roofs of this housing project. And so, in a way, what you're looking at is an image of a landscape on a landscape of roofs, working at a different resolution in a different scale. This is what print media allows you to work with.

Color works also through material and ornament at the same time because it's always moving between two and three dimensions. In 2015, for a Nissan exhibition, entitled *Bust*, we did a project called Face-to-Face. We had to design a bust that was also a house. A bust of course is a human figure, so this gave the elements of the house an anthropomorphic condition. We worked in 3D and then back into 2D. The project goes back into the isolation of the planes and then the coloration defines each one of these flat volumes amongst each other.

One of the other mediums that we work through is form. The way we consider form is between 2D and 3D, and we talk about it in terms of 2.5D. For the Taichung Cultural Center competition, the brief asked for a museum and a library. It specified that the facade on the main street had to be unified, while the library and the museum each had to have distinct qualities. Our proposal was about slicing the form in order to produce tw

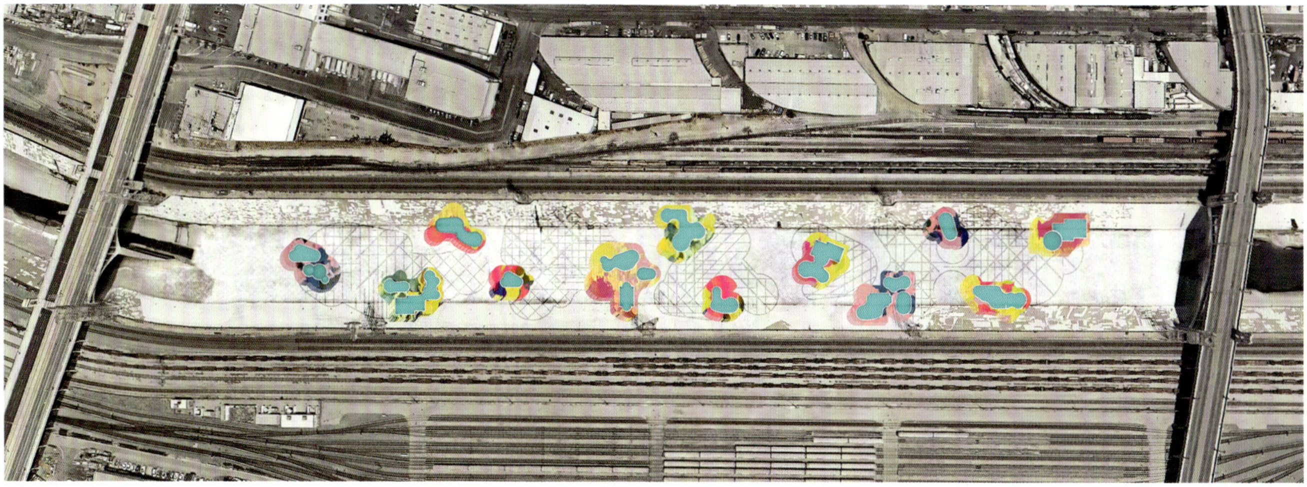

Florencia Pita and Jackilin Hah Bloom, Flat Pools, Los Angeles, CA

different facades—one that unifies the building and one for the museum and the library.

For the Harvey Milk Plaza competition, we proposed a plaza with a three-dimensional outline. We thought about what the street would look like if the plaza were filled with volumes. They would be implied through a space frame that would hold lighting and other amenities. The plaza is typically very dense with people and activity, and we thought about immersive color that would be flattened onto the pavement.

The last topic we want to talk about is curves. We use the word trace to represent curves. One of our projects, called Signatures, looked at how the trace moves from an original to uniqueness. You can see the character of a person and their uniqueness in their signature. Opposed to some of the earlier projects we just presented, where the trace maintains its reference, here the trace of the signature is a trace unto itself. In Signatures, we were working on a two-dimensional image to be placed on to a glass facade at Princeton University. We looked at signature curves, sections of curves, and how they can imply a three-dimensionality. The 2D and 3D can work through partial curvature and start to create volumes. At the same time, they can work through the flatness of their collage. For the image on the glass, we used perforated film so at night, the project reverses and you're only left with the curves.

For Balloon Frame, our proposal for the MoMA PS1 Young Architects Program, we started looking at the Macy's Thanksgiving Day Parade and what the balloons project onto the streets of New York. They create shadow figures that have almost the scale of architecture. We worked through these partial tracings of the balloons themselves and we rearranged

Florencia Pita and Jackilin Hah Bloom, Maribor Housing, Slovenia

them in into new profiles. So, while these profiles start as two-dimensional, they somehow become more material, and then they become structural. The flatness of the profile can become structural by intersecting the curves rather than adding volume. We made our own balloons to create a projected image onto the surface of these arches.

Our work to date has mostly been research- and speculatively-based. But the last two projects we wanted to show are housing projects in Mexico. We're now confronted with issues of economy, social housing, and domesticity. We started to think about how color, form, and curves would play into these projects. One project is in Saltillo, where Edward Hopper used to paint town scenes. The buildings are very low and our prompt, which came from the government housing agency of Mexico, was to build a three-unit apartment building. These are small units but the idea is that this mini-tower would start to propel a densification of the city.

We are also working on a rural house project in Mexico. Here, crisscrossing walls allow for additions, so that family units can add onto the house so that, as a complex, it can grow readily from the center rather than linearly along the street.

The site is currently under construction, being graded, and they will be building 32 prototype houses by 32 different offices.

Florencia Pita and Jackilin Hah Bloom, Taichung City Cultural Center, Taiwan, 2013

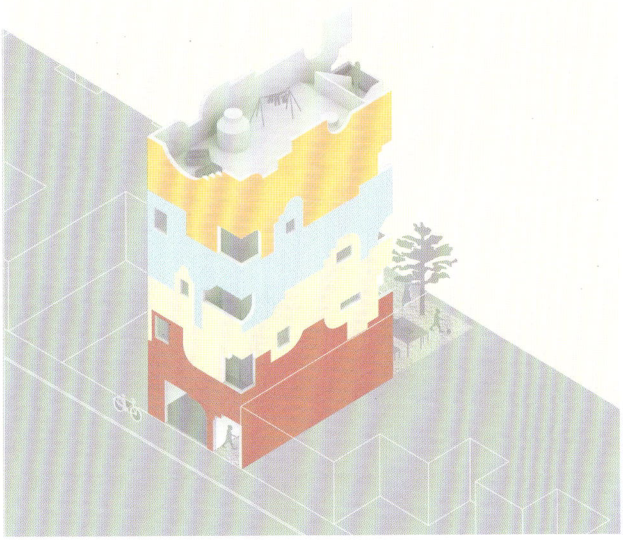

Florencia Pita and Jackilin Hah Bloom, Saltillo Housing, Mexico

Florencia Pita and Jackilin Hah Bloom, Balloon Frame, MoMA PS1, Long Island City, NY, 2014

Florencia Pita and Jackilin Hah Bloom, Shaped Plaza, San Francisco, CA

Florencia Pita and Jackilin Hah Bloom, Balloon Frame, MoMA PS1, Long Island City, NY, 2014

Young & Ayata

NEW YORK, NY

We like to say that one of architecture's responsibilities is the aesthetics of the background of reality. That's pretty loaded, so let's think about what each of those terms means and how we interpret them. By "background," we mean something close to Walter Benjamin's definition of architecture in *The Work of Art in the Age of Mechanical Reproduction* (1936): architecture is an art form that is consumed habitually in a state of distraction by the masses.

Now, as architects we generally don't want to be doing the thing that is consumed habitually in a state of distraction. We want to be doing the thing that is in the foreground. But we've realized that as you walk through your world, most of what you notice you don't notice—it is in the background. Think about how people consume this background; if you can do something to that, you've actually done something incredibly political.

By "aesthetics," we mean the ways in which the world becomes sensible, but it also means the ways in which aesthetics challenge us to have a voice. Who can say what, who can say it where, and what are the ways in which the world can represent itself? Aesthetics are a provocation.

And as far as the word "reality," our interpretation is more akin to realism; the tension that exists between reality and its representation. It is the way in which artworks, through aesthetics, begin to produce a tension that calls you to think differently.

Young & Ayata, Base Flowers, Volume Gallery, Chicago, IL, 2015

Two terms that we want to talk about tonight are abstraction and realism. Usually, we consider these things antithetical. Consider Clement Greenberg's essay "Avant-Garde and Kitsch" (1939). We're still hovering around some of the assumptions embedded in this pairing. With avant-garde, we have abstraction, the forward-looking, the progressive. We have the ways in which culture is being challenged by our artists. With kitsch, we have realism, we have the art for the masses, something that is easy to consume. It is something that is maybe even the construction of propaganda, and it is retrograde.

But is the pairing of avant-garde and kitsch, or abstraction and realism truly antithetical? What we're going to suggest is that within aesthetics, abstraction and realism are not opposites. Within the estrangement of realism, abstraction is one of the things often used. And within the estrangement of abstraction, realism comes in very strange ways.

In 2015, we were asked by Volume Gallery in Chicago to design an object. We became interested in designing a flower vase. There are two problems present in the flower vase. One is architectural: the container needs to recede into the background to bring attention to that which is being contained, presenting the flower as the main object for contemplation. Secondly, we all love flowers, even though they are abstracted and imprisoned pieces of nature. While we contemplate their beauty, they're dying.

These were two points of departure for our Base Flowers series. We were interested in whether there could be a hybrid, and we came up with the idea of a tumbling flower vase; four vessels that were tumbling around to produce different postures. They all had to be contained so they could hold water for the flowers.

As objects, they begin to gain some attitude; they look animalistic. We fabricated them in different materials, but the main ambition was to erase the materiality of the original fabrication to provoke other qualities around the vases in combination with the flowers. Going one step further, if we could take attention away from the binary relationship of the flower and the vase, we could maybe also implant another fiction—the fabrication of a dead flower next to the dying flower. We 3D-printed our own flowers, playing off associated aesthetics of botanical life, like the color and the feel of the surfaces. We curated these flowers in such a way as to camouflage them within the actual nature.

Young & Ayata, Base Flowers, Volume Gallery, Chicago, IL, 2015

Then there was an opportunity to take that fiction a little further. We presented renderings next to the flower vases where you begin to see the anatomical making of these fake flowers. Something is obviously wrong with these flowers. They're overly geometric and digital, perhaps. Nevertheless, you thought you were looking at the real thing. Exploring the fiction at a finer resolution is only possible within the rendering, in the digital medium. Perhaps this would make you go back to the flower vase and re-contemplate what you were just looking at. We wanted to deposit a sense of doubt into what you experienced or what you assumed was real.

In 2016, we participated in an exhibition at the SCI-Arc Gallery, along with Florencia Pita and Jackilin Bloom. It was an invitation to look at the contemporary detail, post-digital fabrication. We decided to reexamine the most ordinary detail—the wall reveal. In most contemporary construction, the reveal is the detail that removes itself; it becomes the shadow line. It fulfills a pragmatic purpose but it also turns the wall into an abstract floating object that has no connection to the surfaces that it adjoins.

We 3D-printed a collection of critters: different wall reveals as an investigation of how to estrange a background moment that hovers within our every day. For the exhibition, we built a construction with four full-scale internal corners in which we jacked four different investigations of these wall reveals. Each of them does something slightly different. One attempted to suck the corner back into the infinity of the interior poche of the wall, as if that could go back again and again. Another looked at how you flutter the corner up and around, allowing the gypsum board to pass through as if the ceiling wasn't there. The third took the geometric constraint at the corners, but put more pressure on those points to locate them in space and cause you to misread the depth of the corner. The fourth was our favorite because it just looked like something really off had happened. Whereas the other three had a certain level of ornamental articulation, the fourth just made the walls look wrong, which was enough for us. It tries to ask a question about the ways in which we establish the aesthetics of the everyday and how we can question them in an alternate matter.

The last project we want to show is a project in Mexico. It is our first building. It's located in a middle-class neighborhood in Mexico City, on a very narrow street in an area that has recently been rezoned. Most new developments here are built up to their plotlines, so we anticipated that our neighbors would eventually also maximize the site area and develop party walls. We offset our design so that we could have a four-sided building that could stand alone. The challenge would be having three narrow corridors surrounding the building—the street front and the sides of the building, which eventually will be built up. The question became how to lay out the apartments so rooms could have access to the views in the back and the street in the front, without anyone directly looking into the building.

This is a mid-market housing project which doesn't allow much play. We had to be incredibly careful about how we incorporated the slightest bit of experimentation. We started with a focus on the apertures to define its character. Turning the windows inward, like a negative bay window into the space itself, allows oblique qualities to emerge.

To make this an interesting project everything would hinge on the execution of these windows. The danger is that if it gets value-engineered, you're left with ugly trapezoidal windows on a flat facade. So, we began to look less at the apertures but at the thickening of the slab itself. If we could get the slab to read as something defamiliarized from how we understand it, we could see the project in a different light and the aperture becomes secondary.

To be smart about this, the formwork had to be reusable and repeatable. It's symmetrical within section and it redeploys itself in different locations. There are five different types. Our initial tests were focused on how to make this in the simplest way of casting concrete. We made the formwork out of straight boards, but realized that using self-settling concrete as a medium is then out of question. So, we looked at the great tradition that exists already, as visible in Félix Candela's work for example: twisted boards would allow us to navigate the issue of the concrete's consistency and it's a technique that locally they

are very familiar with already. However, you have to bend the form to get it out of its place after casting, so we could not use reusable negative wooden formwork. Instead, we constructed the positive form out of wood and produced the negative in carbon fiber, which registered the markings of the wood.

The project was supposed to be a fast track project and they approached it slowly. It allowed us to experiment and to test the potentials of different methods. The final mockup was recently completed with the window in place. There's an incredible effect that we hadn't anticipated within the digital environment. The shape of the window pushes you to one corner, into which you can lean and look outside to see both an oblique view of the street or look back through the outside, inside of the living room. When you see the windows from the outside, the articulation and the oblique present themselves almost as two forms on the surface.

In closing, if our ambition is to think about the background of reality as a potential when it comes to aesthetics of estrangement, this is a larger net we're trying to cast and under which we're trying to operate. Whether the project is large or small, whether the program is institutional or otherwise, this large net allows us to make right turns, left turns, U-turns, and sometimes the wrong turn to make different design and aesthetic decisions, as long as the problem stays focused on the estrangement of background of reality.

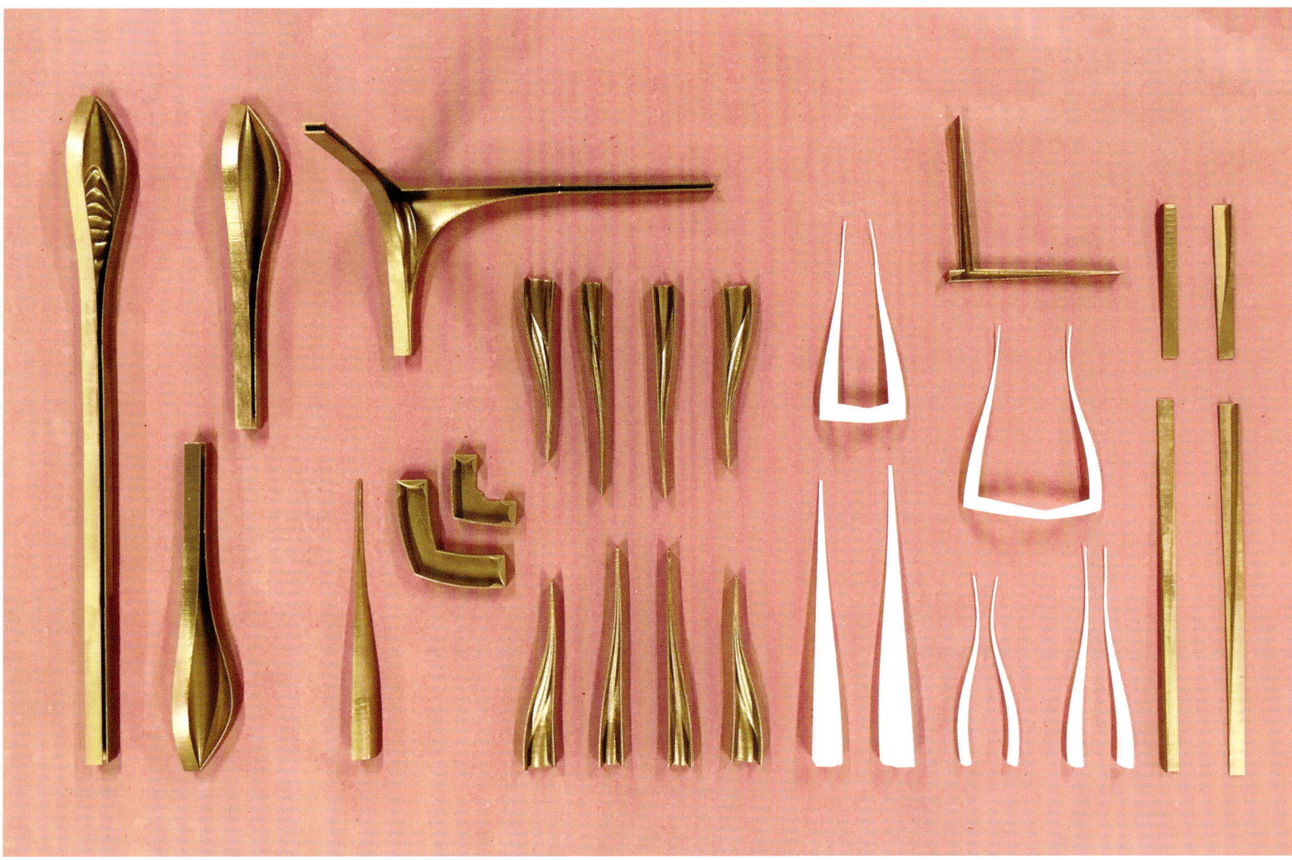

Young & Ayata, Wall Reveal, SCI-Arc Gallery, Los Angeles, CA, 2016

Young & Ayata, Wall Reveal, SCI-Arc Gallery, Los Angeles, CA, 2016

Young & Ayata, DL1310 Apartments, in collaboration with Michan Architecture, Mexico City, Mexico, 2019

Young & Ayata, DL1310 Apartments, in collaboration with Michan Architecture, Mexico City, Mexico, 2019

Conversation

FLORENCIA PITA & JACKILIN HAH BLOOM AND YOUNG & AYATA

David Erdman: We try to use these sessions to develop some precision about how media might be used in the framework of the post-digital. There may be consensus about the fact that it's not limited to the representational- or process-oriented methods of the digital term, but a lot of different language has been used for what the philosophies behind that might be. I have a hard time not seeing the references you are using without invoking direct connection to issues of pictorialism. The way you all work with media is doing weird things to what we might understand to be reality. There is a lot of shared interest in photography and in graphics. Do you think that's a helpful way to sharpen the razor in terms of the discussion of your work or do you think that's too slippery?

Michael Young: Architecture is not a single medium. All the questions about how to become modern, to become critical, to become avant-garde were arguments that dealt with getting specific to your medium and excluding those things that were not pertinent to it. I have a hard time applying that to architecture. So, instead of "medium specificity," we use "medium promiscuity." We are extremely interested in photography and especially a number of contemporary photographers who present, at least initially, a possible or probable world. You look at a photograph and you want to trust it, but then it challenges you in some manner. It shifts your attention. Is that pictorialism? There's somehow an association that I have with pictorialism where it brings me back to questions of the picturesque or questions of whether you are arranging the aesthetics of the architecture to present its primary access through the picture. I don't know if that's something that we agree with in terms of the multiple mediums or the multiple ways of working through design. Is it there? Yes, but for us there is also something that challenges it from multiple mediums. Pictures is one, but the object is another, drawing is a third, and the prototype is a fourth. Together, all of those are building up toward something architectural.

Florencia Pita: It was interesting to see the images of your project in Mexico City because it has a sense of primitivism that I think goes with this idea of medium promiscuity. Pictorialism, the perfection of the image, is gone and it starts to get messy. You're working with the early ways of dealing with material qualities. What you are doing with the wooden formwork for casting concrete, we do with paint, which is the last ingredient that we have left. The complexities of print media that we were looking at within this multi-disciplinary search become the primitivism of construction. That moves away from the image and onto investigations that have to do with material qualities, the role of the drawing against the building, and so on. For our generation, there was a full embrace of technology, but then we have to deal with building things. I think it's an interesting span.

Erdman: The inter-media practices in fine arts started in the 1960s, which also had to do with the integration of technology in an anti-Greenbergian posture. The original pictorialism was a way of giving photography its autonomy, but I'm suggesting a new pictorialism because while you are acknowledging that you're working in intermedia practices, there's a huge amount of disciplinary anxiety about that. There's a Greenbergian hangover that architecture's only medium is space. One way to overcome these anxieties is to consider how we are working with it differently than contemporary photographers might be. It's not reasserting a Greenbergian autonomy, but it's saying that we're all inter-media practices. Is that a way out of the constraints and the trappings of architecture? What I like about both of your practices is that you use it as a way back in, rather than a way out. You're not trying to become fine artists or photographers, but you're using this in very weird ways that only an architect might do.

Jackilin Bloom: It's also about where the criticality is coming from. The tension is in who is setting up the parameters for the way in which the work can be perceived. Most of the time, through architecture, I think we're working through pictorialism in the micro-material: in the color of the materiality or a digital line as a kind of material. That sort of pictorialism is present in both of our works, but not the type of pictorialism that looks at a final image of the project.

Erdman: I think there's a latent history of architects testing inter-media and being promiscuous that somehow hasn't been part of the legacy of how things like drawing and rendering are talked about.

Young: At one level, there are young architects that are convinced that using a rendering or using photography is somehow suspect and we don't participate in it. Renderings can be used to create spectacles and confusions, but they're

also part of the ways in which we communicate, develop, and explore our own designs. At that level, we are interested in the image, without a doubt. Currently there are five or six exhibitions on drawing on view at various locations. When you go to these shows, one of the questions that you're left with is, how are we defining drawing right now? Is it defined through projection? Is it defined through the presence of line? I think every architecture student needs to ask, what are the things we're hanging on to? What are the things we're losing? What are the ways in which we use aesthetics and representation to make arguments? What possible conventions have we been working through in our history that allowed us to make those arguments, and which ones do we need to push forward to make the arguments we're working with today? Drawing can be one of the ways in which we produce dispersive arguments about our work.

Sanford Kwinter, in the audience: If you were to put on the table today an urgent argument, what would that be?

Young: Well, here's the thing, I think we're working on multiple projects that we're trying to figure out, one of which is the project of our office, examining where we sit within the explorations, the design work, the representations, the writings that we produce around that. And I would love to be able to say that I could clearly articulate what the "project" of Young & Ayata is. It's probably a problem that I can't clearly articulate that.

Pita: One problem that we are trying to address is the issue of the "easy." Much of our work has a quality of lightness. It has been called cartoonish, childish, and feminine. It has been called many things, so we have embraced that as a topic.

From left to right: David Erdman, Michael Young, Jackilin Hah Bloom, Kutan Ayata, and Florencia Pita in conversation at Pratt Sessions 8.

It's easy to absorb much of that work and yet it's very difficult to attain. It's difficult to construct. It's very elaborate and tedious. We are teaching a studio about that topic right now. Consider Andy Warhol, who looked at the easiness of popular culture of the everyday. He absorbed this and then re-presented it back to us through his art in ways that were compelling. With all of the methods that we use in our work—coloring, paint by numbers, and different methodologies—we similarly try to absorb consumer culture in an easy manner, while also being very elaborate with a close reading.

Erdman: If you had to talk about something that's urgent, I would think both your firms would look at how graphic designers and visualization firms could start taking over most of our work. Part of the problem you seem to be working through is how you get back some of that territory for architecture firms. What you're doing has other haptic and qualitative attributes to it that a graphic designer wouldn't be capable of expounding upon. You're not running away from media, which some architects do. Nor does your work suggest that it's jumping ship and becoming photography or fine art. Rather, it occupies a very uncomfortable and challenging territory that's suggesting, "We're going to work with it, but in a way that builds upon disciplinary themes in architecture." It's urgent and it has a push behind it that may not be totally evident, because the way you're doing it requires a deep sophistication.

Kwinter: David is right, of course. I also felt that both offices would probably explain that they were somehow interested in engaging the problem of contemporary experience. In both your work, there is a recognition that there was something quite toxic going on and that architecture is meant to save our brain, our mind, and our soul from these things and find new forms of engagement. There are a lot of implicit arguments present in the work.

Young: I think there's a political argument in this if we distinguish between a close reading and a close attention project. In one, you work through the different mechanisms and representations to decode the symbolic or linguistic artifacts of architecture, referencing it to history, geometry, precedent, and to modes of organization that have become part of what we learn as architects. In the other, you challenge the articulation of the architecture so that it drives you to pay attention to it in a different mode. Is that color? Is it taking a typical typology and altering it in some manner? Is it taking something that you assume to be one way and then it is subverting those expectations? Many of our projects develop an interior that's radically different than the exterior. And we are incredibly focused on making sure that the project negotiates that transition between interiority and exteriority.

Kwinter: So, you would say, the answer to my first question is that you're interested in giving place to the attentional rather than the historical reading?

Erdman: What is interesting about the attentiveness is that you can say that the way a graphic design firm designs an environment for Samsung or Apple is focused on stimulation in an effort to develop consumption. This is a different strategy of design from attentiveness, which you could identify as being more architectural. Somehow that attentiveness is designed and that might be a way to argue for a mediatric promiscuity that still has to do with the very specific architectural traits, distinguishing it from stimulation or distraction.

Audience question: The notion of the foreground and the background seems such a perfect way of putting this dilemma. It cannot be in the foreground because it becomes spectacle, and it cannot recede fully into the background, because it will disappear. So, how do we tease it out? Both these practices do that in very different ways. It seems to me that it is just the politics of today in a kind of rather straightforward way. Good or bad, it seems to be the hand of cards that we've been dealt. Would you agree or do you believe that our role is still the avant-garde notion of disciplinary progress?

Kutan Ayata: There is not one umbrella under which we can gather an architectural attitude. From west coast to east coast, from north to south, everybody is going in different directions, and it seems impossible to establish a singular project to follow. We find that incredibly exciting. There are multiple politics and trajectories within this. We are comfortable having completely different attitudes about architecture and design. That kind of multiplicity for me is refreshing. Within these various directions, we can make different turns. Are we rigorous and serious? I hope so. Are we political? Perhaps secretly, perhaps indirectly. I just don't see the validity of a singular, large project.

Audience question: But is there still a belief in how disciplinary progress was defined for the last 120 years? Is there an ideology that's either driven by technological advancement and how that filters into cultural expressions, or are we occupying a state of pluralism that may be personally liberating, but in terms of a larger disciplinary effort, also potentially problematic?

Pita: I would say that the radical project is not a project. I think the 1968 generation killed that project for us. The revolutionary drawings and concepts built up a revolution within.

Audience question: The 1990s project was not radical?

Pita: No, Patrik Schumacher killed it for us. He tried to make the digital project radical, he tried to convert it to an *-ism*. It completely transformed architecture, but in those earlier projects, you'll find more qualities that challenged architecture.

We have to look for new sources of inspiration and I think that's the difficulty of the digital project today. I think that that's why we look in the background. We go back to Walter Benjamin for rescue.

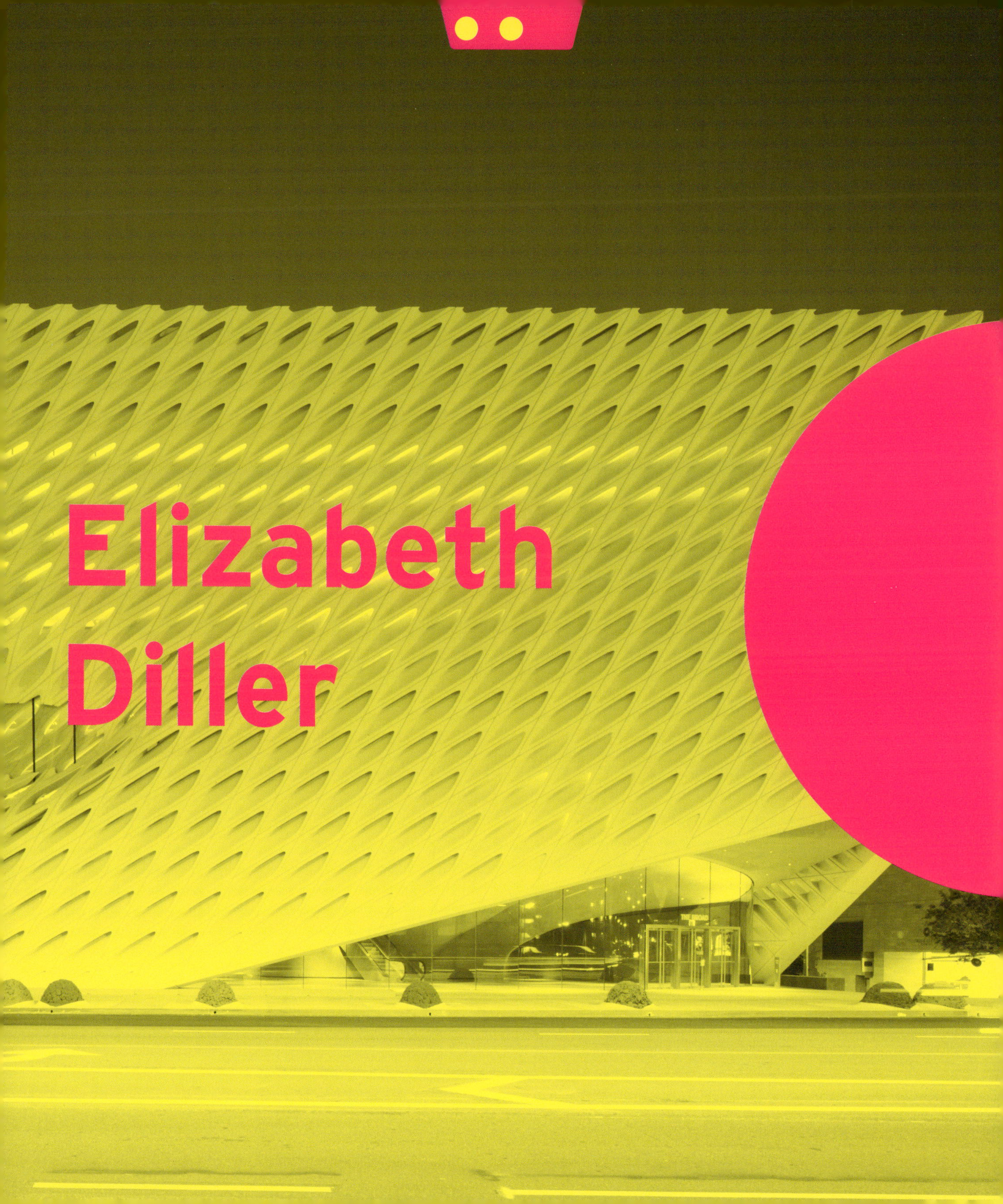
Elizabeth
Diller

Sylvia
Lavin

02

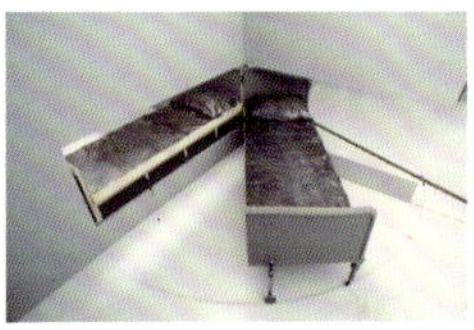

03

06

08

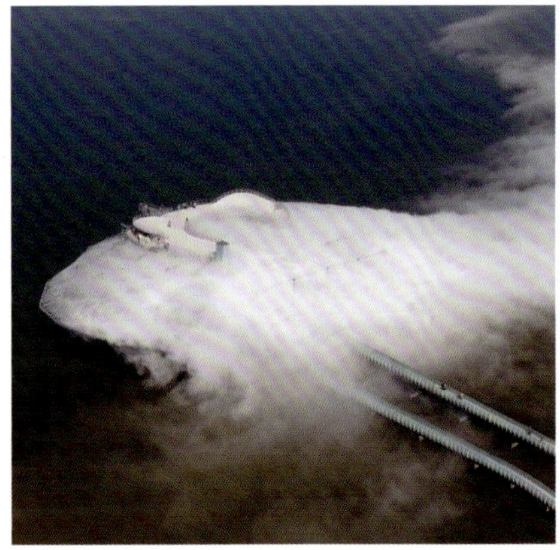

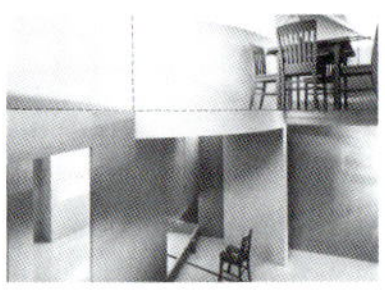

01

04

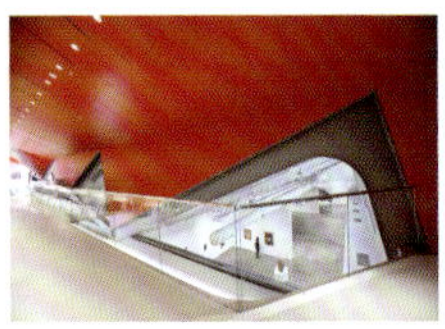

05

07

09

10

11

15

17

12

13

14

16

Introduction

DAVID ERDMAN

Tonight, we're joined by Elizabeth Diller and Sylvia Lavin, two of the foremost progenitors of contemporary discourse and the discussion on architectural mediums.

Diller Scofidio + Renfro is a nimble architectural practice. They engage a number of modalities and methods to develop and execute projects. They're experts at intermedia design and have tested it within the various milieus of their work.

Distinctive is the specific inversions of scales and the multiplicities of temporalities in the ways that they tinker with perceived media. Drawings become rooms, rooms become drawings. **01** Rotation and section become actualized mechanics, transforming space. **02** "Oculi," "mirrors," and "windows" infuse spatial dislocations or collapse certain durations into architectural frameworks and mass. **03** "Iteration" becomes artifacted, cut through objects, marking and bifurcating space and time into other dimensions. **04**

The sensate and the olfactory are also things that they have worked with. All of these mediums are compressed into one unadulterated architectural obsession and device: the section. In their work the section measures and marks architectural tempo. It entwines representational and live media, and forms a highly-mediated topology of time and space. **05**

Lastly, distinctive in their work is the use of screens, something we all live with daily and might understand as the canonical medium to deliver mediated communications. **06** Screens are evident and exposed in their architectural work, past and present. A colossal cyclops seems to be luring in many of the projects. It is gazing upon you and instead of you looking at the screen, which might be how most of us think about our subjective disposition to media, it might be looking at and surveying you. **07**

This discourse on the screen is taken literally in new conceptions of media facades, where exteriors become mediums that have vivid and alternative qualities—thick and vaporous, rough and granulated, taught and elastic. **08** **09**

What is perhaps the most shocking effect of the work Liz has been doing with Diller Scofidio + Renfro is the way in which architecture binds communication and content to various mediums: plastic, water, plants, screens. More often than not, this is *not* done through text, but through the building responding to you. It might creep up on you or envelop you.

Akin to Stanislaw Lem's, *Solaris* (1961), where the ocean has consciousness and is alive, the composite of synthetic media and natural mediums of representational and live media in Diller Scofidio + Renfro's work imbues the architecture with a different sense of character. No longer in the tradition of stylistic or aesthetic character, this is arguably new. The architecture is behavioral, interactive, psychological, and live; perhaps we might discuss tonight the extent to which it's *alive*.

Sylvia Lavin is a formidable critic and theoretician. Her writing and curatorial work continues to set the stage for contemporary thinking, architectural interdisciplinarity, and their potential formats or cultural affiliations. She has a razor-sharp acuity that affords her the capability to flip over conventional presumptions, histories, and sentiments in a manner that opens up productive new territory within architecture discourse, and beyond.

With an air of eroticism, wit, unparalleled rigor, and depth, her work has allowed us to understand abstract formalism as a tool for psychoses. **10** Thus, the abstract is reoriented toward the flippant, the moody, and the affective.

Sylvia has taken expendable materials like plastic, promiscuous in its ability to form anything and the antagonist of architecture's permanence, and re-orchestrated entire veins of disciplinarity and history along that material's lexical trajectory.

Sylvia is supercharged. She is hot pink with silver letters and her work on media is electric and dazzling. **11** Like a sucker punch to the gut, her arguments seemingly manifest out of nowhere and drive deep. The most innocent of gestures, a kiss, becomes a surgical weapon, striking hard at the striations and divisions between art and design disciplines. It imbues interior and exterior, media and architecture with a productive and confounded semi-autonomy that affords them a degree of political and cultural prowess.

Her writing and tenor have a brevity and precision that is truly astounding. **12** Ideas spark in your mind when you read her work.

Whether it's a collection of proto-digital representational drawings, back lit or blistering with color, fragments of buildings and models that polka dot a room, the exhibitions she has curated make their contents live. **13** Drawings become installations, full-scale details of buildings become kaleidoscopic

arrays of objects to circumnavigate. 14 15 The space is full, immersing one into the content, requiring one to get up close and personal with it. 16 The boundary between content and the reader is diminished. 17

Important to this evening's discussion is the way in which she has anchored and evolved a discourse on the media we find ingrained into architectural space; removing them from their confinement as solely representational and exploiting their potentials at full scale.

Sylvia gives us an understanding and the courage to engage other modalities of design in specifically architectural ways, through color, luminosity, graphics, and painting, by making them a vital and necessary aspect of the live experience and vibratory qualities of architecture.

While Liz and Sylvia are two of the foremost progenitors of the contemporary discussion on architectural mediums, they come from differing perspectives: Liz is a designer whose work and interests have actively engaged a multitude of media, and Sylvia's writing has elucidated poignant and provocative theories regarding how architecture's historic (and contemporary) inclusion, collusion, rejection, and confounded interrelatedness to media may be worthy of our attention today.

A key thing we are trying to explore here in the GAUD is not so much that these media and mediums are new either as technologies nor praxes that have overlapped with design. Clearly the communicative aspect of media (mass media in particular) has deeply influenced architecture discourse and its visual culture. Art criticism and theory have equally influenced our discourse on mediums—abstract or otherwise.

What is new-ish, though not without deep historic and disciplinary roots, is the willing contamination of media in architecture (allowing them to push back on the building), as well as the intentional design of their interdimensional and temporal cadences—binding them to live experience. These are the foundations of intermedia practices.

From Van Doesburg through the Eames and Venturi, one can see the hints and glimmers of bringing signage, media, and art/design-based mediums into the realm of architecture. Designers and thinkers—including our two guests—have been probing these matters. Architects have been testing the waters, embracing media, introducing a range of media facade types from signs to bushes to clouds.

And clearly here in New York City we are well poised to investigate this—not only because of our history of using architecture as signaling and communicative devices, but also because of current opportunities to rethink those models; making them more lively, and perhaps even establishing new concepts of "character."

Let's see how the presentations and discussions bring some of this together.

Elizabeth Diller

NEW YORK, NY

As there are two theorists that are going to be presenting tonight, Sylvia and Catherine, I'm going to do the thing that I promised myself I wouldn't do way back, which is to just show some work. I don't have a theory, but I just compiled a sampling of media as a prompt.

We recently did a project called Musings on a Glass Box, which was done for the Fondation Cartier Pour L'Art Contemporain in Paris in honor of the thirtieth anniversary of Jean Nouvel's building there. The building features two side-by-side galleries with floor-to-ceiling glass. What does an architect do to celebrate the thirtieth anniversary of another architect's building?

The idea was to play with some of the things that don't go right in architecture, like leaks, plumbing, glazing, and some of the electricity that's running through the building. I wanted to use those modalities and figure out something to do with it. The central protagonist was a bucket, bought at a local hardware store. It was smart and figured out where the leaks were, moving there before the droplet fell from the ceiling. The glass walls of the gallery were pulsing, transitioning from transparent to opaque with LCD panels.

Inside the bucket, we installed a bucket cam. The camera looked at the ceiling to figure out where to go next. We wanted

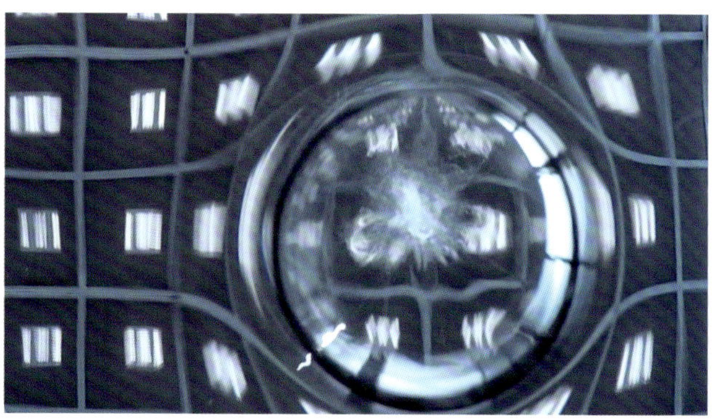

Diller Scofidio + Renfro, Musings on a Glass Box, Fondation Cartier, Paris, France, 2015

Diller Scofidio + Renfro, Musings on a Glass Box, Fondation Cartier, Paris, France, 2015

to accentuate the drop of water so that was more than just a drop. We added an amplifying device to really hear the drop hit the bucket.

In the next room, a huge monitor hung close to the floor. The only way you could get under it to see the screen was on a mechanical dolly, like the one that a mechanic uses to get under cars. The screen showed the feed from the camera inside the bucket. You would see this image on a gigantic scale, and you hear the sound.

We asked David Lang to compose the sound of that droplet. The droplet was actual, but the resonance was something that he prerecorded, sung by human singers. David wanted to make this space feel like a cathedral. That was really what you felt. The grotesque image was very psychedelic and then you heard this beautiful sound.

A very new project for us is The Shed. In 2008, the City of New York issued an RFP for a cultural institution or entity in the redevelopment site of Hudson Yards. Of course, 2008 was a very bad time in the economy and nobody was thinking about new institutions. With David Rockwell, our partner on this, we asked ourselves the question of what New York needs that it doesn't yet have. What kind of cultural institution could happen on this site? New York has a lot of cultural institutions: museums, galleries, theaters, and performance spaces. But it doesn't really have a place that's purpose-built for visual arts, the performing arts, creative industry, and pop culture. Our idea was that this new institution could generate income for itself. It would have produced, co-produced, and presented events, as well as income-generating events.

We were selected to go forward; we might have been the only ones that applied. We started to study what this could

Diller Scofidio + Renfro, The Shed, New York, NY, 2019

really be. We imagined this as being about flexibility. There would be a static base building, a stack of large floor plates, column-free galleries that could host anything. On an adjacent empty site, there would be indoor and outdoor programming. An expandable, telescoping shell would come onto the site to almost double the footprint of the fixed building.

The only source of inspiration that we had was the Fun Palace (1959-1961) by Cedric Price, which was an architecture of infrastructure, like ours. It was basically a combination of loading capacity, electrical power, and space. We used industrial-coined technologies, re-purposed and rethought for a new structure.

We had a meeting with the Mayor, who asked, "Do you have a business plan for this?" While we had previously had the idea about The Shed being self-sustainable, this was the first time we ever thought about how to actually do it. In the end, we were talked into taking over the base of the residential building next door. All our back-of-house space—our storage, offices, mechanical equipment, and all that—is located there.

The simple base building is a framed structure, and the movable shed is actually built up from the wheels with the steel rising from six points, then crossing over and becoming rigid. There are loading docks on 30th Street, so trucks can drive directly into the building to unload. This allows different ways of hosting large flexible events and installations. We can haul a Richard Serra up to the third floor, for example. The Shed space can be darkened so you can use it as a space to show films. It comes with sound isolation, so you can have concerts or host Fashion Week.

We've had to pitch this to many different people along the

way, but in the end, the City decided this was a good idea and they helped fund this. Now it is a non-profit institution, independent of the City.

We did a lot of technical work and analysis on this project, such as a glare analysis and examining the way the air moves. The sidewalls of the shed are a structure of ETFE pillows and large guillotine doors that open and close to allow flexibility between inside and outside. When the doors are shut, it's thermally tight so you can do anything you want to, anytime of year. We had to convince the New York City Department of Buildings to allow us not to paint everything with intumescent paint.

The motors that drive the movable shed are at the top of the base building. The two sets of motors equal one Prius engine. So, it's very energy efficient and it takes five minutes to deploy the building.

I just keep thinking, how could this possibly have happened? It has a different business plan now, but the building is largely the same as it was before.

Diller Scofidio + Renfro, Musings on a Glass Box, Fondation Cartier, Paris, France, 2015

Diller Scofidio + Renfro, The Shed, New York, NY, 2019

Diller Scofidio + Renfro, Musings on a Glass Box, Fondation Cartier, Paris, France, 2015

Diller Scofidio + Renfro, Musings on a Glass Box, Fondation Cartier, Paris, France, 2015

Sylvia Lavin

PRINCETON, NJ

Liz and I had an interesting conversation where we realized that we were unsure whether tonight was supposed to be about mediums or media. That's an interesting slip of technology and disciplinary tongue. How can we think about contemporary media and the idea of a medium? To me, interesting new media are things like open source GoogleDocs and how they move through the world. We recently saw the publication and circulation of the "Shitty Men in Architecture" GoogleDoc. There, architecture meets the #MeToo movement through the media of the open source shared doc, where anybody can say anything about anybody. This public forum works on the honor system, where public scrutiny of what you put up is supposed to be truthful.

I was thinking that most people would say, "Well, the GoogleDoc is an interesting media, but it has nothing to do with architecture itself, so why is she talking about this?" My focus in this presentation is going to be the idea of "architecture itself." The last 30 years, architecture itself has been how we understand the architectural medium.

Peter Eisenman is one of the architects included in this list of GoogleDoc cells, but his entries are largely empty. This is not the first time that Eisenman has been subjected to a new media-driven critique. The way in which he would be criticized for certain things is historically specific. This idea of architecture itself begins with Eisenman's essay "Notes on Conceptual Architecture" (1970), which, amongst other things, is about Giuseppe Terragni and his House of Fascism (1932-1936). It's an essay in which fascism is in fact never mentioned, except in the name of the building. In this way, the essay performs a radical divide between some notion of architecture as a political thing and architecture itself.

In 1974, Eisenman presented his class at Cooper Union with a copy of his article as a take-home essay test. One of his students was Liz Diller, who wrote at the end of the essay,

> "It would be a futile attempt to even raise objections as my perceptions and my conceptions are not as developed as yours. For that matter, I do not believe you are asking for opinions, but a rephrasing of already made definitions and philosophies. So, in the hopes that the purpose of all this is learning, I've decided to give you the information anyway, but in its least adulterated form."

In other words, Liz gave Peter back to Peter and circled in pencil the parts in which Peter was the least adulterated.

The pencil and the Xerox copy may be Liz Diller's first piece of conceptual art and it happens in a critique of Peter Eisenman's work. Part of what is at stake is the idea of architecture itself. His text, her Xerox machine, and her pencil start to do a certain kind of work. I'm trying to suggest that architecture itself, which we believe does not have anything to do with the GoogleDoc but that is in fact a condition of this idea of architecture itself that presents itself as an a-historical notion of a medium, is actually quite historically specific. We can begin to understand its emergence in the mid-1960s through the technologies and media that generated discourse at that time.

Colin Rowe wrote a statement when looking to get support from the Graham Foundation to publish his essays. At the bottom, Rowe argues, "Please support me because I want to talk about the continuing nature of architecture as such." He doesn't say what "architecture as such" is, but he goes on to say what it is not. It is not the notion of modernity as an independent force; it is not the notion of the architect as hero; it is not about image making; it is not architecture presented as the product of modern conditions of production; it is not architecture reduced to photographs and image-making.

Rowe is trying to produce the idea that "architecture as such" is something else. He never says that it is something like "architecture as geometry." He makes this argument when he first publishes "Mathematics of the Ideal Villa" in 1974. It's based

Installation shot of *Architecture Itself and Other Postmodern Myths* exhibition, curated by Sylvia Lavin, Canadian Centre for Architecture (CCA), 2018-2019

Jesse Reiser. Copy of composition with the Modena Cemetery by Aldo Rossi, Drawing Matter Somerset, 1979

on the format of a lecture with slide-by-slide presentations. It is the media setup of the classroom at the time that enables him to do things like place Palladio and Le Corbusier in the same universe, as though that were not an act of an incredible magician. He learned this magic act, of course, from his teacher, Rudolf Wittkower, who also spoke elaborately with these slide projection lectures. Wittkower himself was a kind of magician, taking all of the specificities of Palladio, drawing them again and again until they turned into the nine-square grid.

That nine-square grid then required the erasure not only of Palladio and his specifics, but of these extraordinary drawings by Wittkower, where he is somehow conflating a replica of Palladio's book and the building, trying to make a measured drawing. I'm interested in this process of erasure. Part of what I'm describing here is a "double set of books."

In the postwar period, corporate culture started to develop a financial strategy that gets called "the double set of books." Normally, when we use that phrase we think something untoward is happening, but in fact keeping two sets of books is a totally legal corporate structure. To the IRS you want to minimize your assets so that you pay the least amount of taxes; to your corporate board you show the maximum assets because you need to show that you're actually making some money. The corporate world is completely comfortable with the idea that any financial situation is internally divided and addresses different audiences with different sets of facts.

Peter Eisenman is the architectural master of the double set of books for a variety of reasons. The essay that he asked his students to read was first published in *Design Quarterly*, but nobody ever read it. Why would you? The first page was essentially blank, so as a reader you got the idea on the first page and you went to the next article. No one ever looked at the second page, which said that you were supposed to write to the Institute of Architecture and Urban Studies and have Peter send you the full text. I spent a lot of time in the archives of the Institute, I can find no evidence that one person ever asked for the text. The text failed to circulate, and therefore had to be published as the form that was then given to Liz as a student.

I'm interested in establishing a theory of architecture as the theory of the cover-up, negotiating the problem of the double set of books. The history of architecture from the 1970s onward is full examples of this, and the ingenuity of the cover up is just delicious. In 1977, Leo Castelli Gallery hosted the *Architecture One* show. It included Aldo Rossi's drawings of the Modena Cemetery. He was hoping to sell them in the commercial gallery. Meanwhile, as this is happening, he's walking around the halls of Cooper Union and looking over the desk of students like Jesse Reiser. Rossi hires Jesse to make a copy of his Modena Cemetery drawing. In the lower left it says "Composition of Modena Cemetery 1972" and next to it, "School of Aldo Rossi 1979, copy by Jesse Reiser." It's the most extraordinary, guilt-ridden confession that you could possibly imagine.

A few years later, Michael Graves was entering the Portland Building competition, which required an artistry of presentation, but also required boards to be submitted in multiples. How do you produce 40 copies of a Michael Graves drawing for a competition? Well, you turn to the Xerox machine and color your copies in by hand. With Michael, it's so extraordinary what he does with the Xerox machine that the anonymous mode of reproduction and the highly personal art overlay, or in our case the GoogleDoc and architecture itself, become so entangled that he doesn't even recognize the distinction between them.

Installation shot of *Architecture Itself and Other Postmodern Myths* exhibition, curated by Sylvia Lavin, Canadian Centre for Architecture (CCA), 2018-2019

To conclude, Peter Eisenman gave Liz an F. The thing that's most amazing to me is that he kept her paper. Why keep a record of what must be understood as a colossal blunder?

In 1975, Eisenman completed his House VI. He hired an airplane pilot to fly over the house to take an aerial photograph. Peter then had the photograph airbrushed, taking out the landscape, pipes, and a whole series of other things in order to try to make the photograph look like a model. Because, of course, architecture itself is cardboard. It's a pure idea. What I love the most about this is the conversation that I had with Peter about it, in which he kept saying, "No, actually it's a photograph of a model." No, Peter, actually it's not. You have now believed your own Kool-Aid.

The great ingenuity of architecture of the last 30 years has been to try to negotiate these new technologies and the need to have multiple sets of books. And it's in the funny gaps in between them where interesting things like puddles, leaks, and so forth emerge.

Installation shot of *Architecture Itself and Other Postmodern Myths* exhibition, curated by Sylvia Lavin, Canadian Centre for Architecture (CCA), 2018-2019

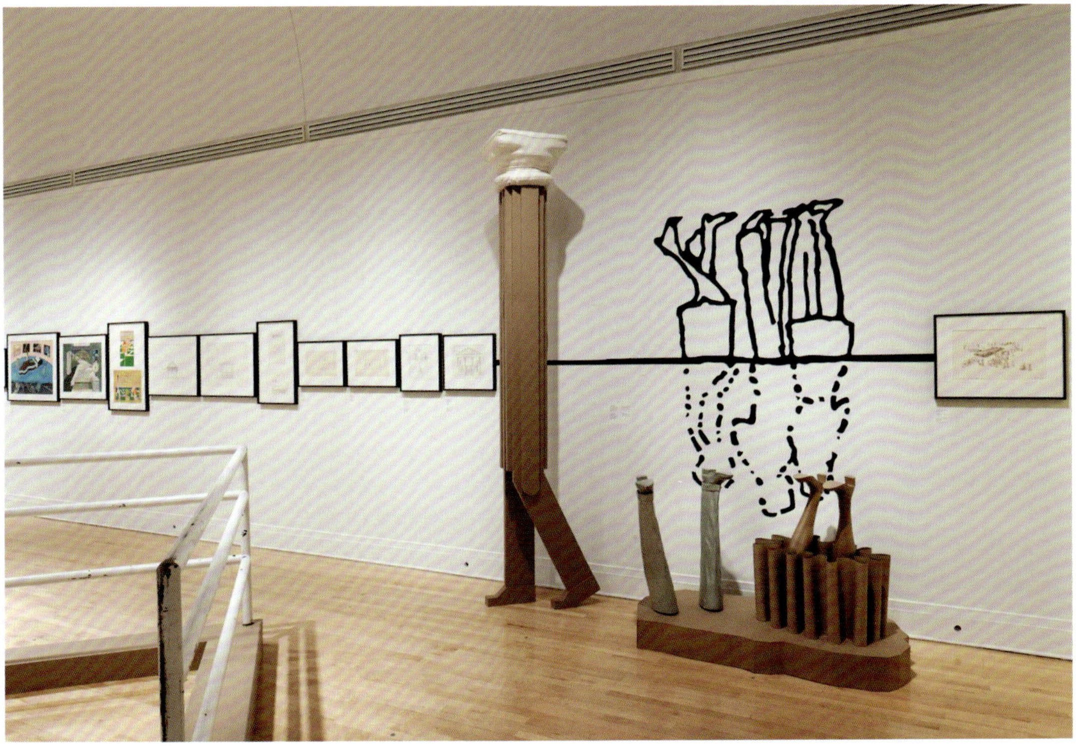

Installation shot of *Architecture Itself and Other Postmodern Myths* exhibition, curated by Sylvia Lavin, Canadian Centre for Architecture (CCA), 2018-2019

Conversation

SYLVIA LAVIN AND ELIZABETH DILLER MODERATED BY CATHERINE INGRAHAM

Catherine Ingraham: Having Liz and Sylvia as a pairing is an extraordinary thing. They're colleagues, they're friends, and they have formulated their work in relationship to each other in many cases.

I want to talk about two projects—Liz's The Shed and Sylvia's exhibition, *The Duck and the Document: True Stories of Postmodern Procedures*, a show at UCLA in 2017, which presented building artifacts and notebooks of thousands of pages of construction documents and correspondence about buildings. I was trying to put this in the context of how Heidegger talks about technology. In his late work, he says that technology is not what we think it is. He has a way of bringing us into this problem. First, he establishes what you thought technology was, then in the next sentence he takes you one step further away from what you thought it was. Then you go back and remind yourself about what you thought it was, and then you go two more steps away from what you thought it was. You gradually get into some other domain altogether, which has curious characteristics that aren't about the technology that we think we know, but in fact, they are about how technology becomes what Heidegger calls "a standing reserve."

The question of the cover-up is important. What is The Shed doing when it moves back and forth over this more stable "standing reserve" of a building? It's fantastic to think of The Shed as a supplement that brings money into the static building; it is about the acquisition of more space, but temporarily you only hold the space with those tracks. The way in which The Shed is built, it has a character that suggests that it wants to leave, as if it were fleeing the standing reserve in favor of something else. It goes out and it holds something that is not the standing reserve.

In the same sense, the documents in Sylvia's exhibition reveal the bureaucracy of architecture. Endless pages are required to bring about architecture itself. That seems to speak to the sense in which we expect buildings to be useful, meaningful, and functional. That struck me as the standing reserve of architecture. On the other hand, the artifacts are doing what The Shed is doing. They're not showing how to use anything, they're sitting there as decorative elements.

The great danger of technology is that we'd become standing reserves ourselves. What Heidegger says is that we see what is revealed by technology and we reflect on it. In this way, The Shed becomes the reflective mechanism that looks back at the standing reserve building and sees what's revealed there. In performative ways, it might bring the building into a more reflective place. The same would be true of these clumsy building artifact pieces in Sylvia's exhibition. They will bring us back to something that is reflective on the documents.

This dynamic between parts is filled with revelations, cover-ups, and ways in which we mistake one for the other. Without any utopian comments about how art will allow us to survive technology, I would like to see if this interpretation rings any bells.

Sylvia Lavin: A couple things: first, I'm trying to become more historically circumscribed in the way that I understand things, which is to say I probably wouldn't read Heidegger anymore for his truth value. I would read Heidegger in relation to the way he was read by phenomenologists in a particular period. I feel safer there these days, given the utter abstractions of the world of Trump. Secondly, the cover-up emerged as a historical concept. The way you managed the facts was more dangerous than whatever the facts were. It's the cover-up that's actionable.

I entered architecture in an era in which public discourse was tainted by this idea of the cover-up. Liz's paper to Peter is all about the question, "Are we on the honor system? You asked me for an opinion, but actually, you wanted your opinion." It was the duplicity with which Eisenman had posed the question that was the problem in the exchange. At a certain moment, architecture entered a space in which it was dealing with itself in terms of a cover-up.

By the way, Peter Eisenman for me is a signifier. I care about the things that Eisenman stands for. There is a photograph of Eisenman sitting across a table from John Portman. It is evidence of a battle that they had where Eisenman is basically saying to Portman, "You're not an architect, you're a developer."

I started reading some more on Portman, because no teacher of mine ever said Portman wrote anything. But in fact, Portman had something very interesting to say. He said, "Most architects think a design begins with a designed sketch. I decided that design begins when somebody has the idea that a building could go there, and the way you express the idea that a building could go there is writing a real estate pro forma."

I don't know if that's right, but it's certainly not stupid. There's an incredible design in the pro forma. Look at The Shed. It begins with an idea that a thing could work in a certain way.

Elizabeth Diller: I have to confess that my very first job was for John Portman, in my first year of architecture school. Thinking about what an architect's role is might have started with John Portman, and I never thought about that until now. What do architects do anyway? I came to a certain point where I thought that just working out programs that were received was not interesting enough. Why not be your own client? That's hard to do if you don't have the money. So, you have to work for other people. But how do you do that in a clever way and create your own context. If the context isn't there, you just make it. In the terrible financial moment of 2008, the aesthetic idea, the programmatic idea, the economic idea, and the cultural idea were all the same thing. The moving structure of The Shed came out of the opportunity to produce something more than it was. I want to talk about the cover-up a little bit. There are so many different manifestations of an idea. Whether it is in the form of models, drawings, texts, renderings, pitches, or post-occupancy documents, they're all new opportunities to think about this thing. Peter didn't want to reveal that he hired a plane and a pilot to generate his image of House VI. He wanted the model and the real thing to be the same, so he made this image. Is that not something that is a willful, creative thing, no matter how Peter wants to talk about it?

David Erdman: To come back to how Sylvia began her presentation: we like to productively conflate media and

From left to right: David Erdman, Sylvia Lavin, Catherine Ingraham, and Elizabeth Diller in conversation at Pratt Sessions 9.

mediums here, at Pratt. The mask, the filter, the touch up—these are things we use in Photoshop. The mask was, certainly in the early 1970s, an architectural strategy for operating on buildings and covering them up to some extent. It's a way of pushing the project forward. The interesting thing about the cover-up is that one could presume that there's a truth behind it. Or we live in the time of multiple cover-ups, where the fake is potentially the real.

Ingraham: How can cover-up be new? I understand that there are new formats for it, but didn't modernism cover up the fact that it was extremely ornamental? It claimed this minimalist mission, but it turns out the I-beams are all custom made, burnished to this beautiful patina, and they become as ornamental as the baroque.

Lavin: Lying is not a modern invention, but the shift in the amount of evidence of crimes and, therefore, the amount of time that would have to be spent in covering them up is a technologically and historically determined phenomenon. However, this is a historical era that we can date from around 1973 to maybe the early 2000s. Now we are in a different era. The GoogleDoc admits of no cover-up. The point of the GoogleDoc is that it exposes everything.

It's in the cover-up that the last era was the most creative and interesting, because the anxiety of being found out restrained them from their unabashedly heroic self-indulgence. That's why I discussed the edited photograph of Eisenman's House VI. This is a whole instrument that involves the airbrush, the airplane, the cardboard, the building; it's totally genius. I did not mean to be ungenerous and to say that there's just a guilty crime. But there was a kind of false confidence during this time, that if you report everything, truth will be permanent. And then suddenly this turned around and became problematic. If everything is written down and the double books are kept, there's no wiggle room.

Diller: In 1999, we did a performance project called, Jet Lag. It was about this real-life character, Donald Crowhurst, who was an electrician that decided to do a yacht race around the world. He was regarded as a great hero because he was like everyman, with a totally unequipped boat, going up against professional sailors. The BBC gave him equipment to put on his boat to do an auto-documentary. He recorded fantastic footage on 16 millimeter. This was before GPS and he was doing radio communications, where he gave false locations of his position. He was basically sailing in circles, he wasn't going anywhere. Ultimately, his boat was capsized and he was never found. They did find his boat, where they also found this other set of books, which were his actual points and locations. This was a moment in time where you could deceive. Today, it's impossible to cover anything up.

There is beauty in the double set of books because, as Sylvia mentioned, it is completely legal. There is a sense of fiction in the real. In architecture, does that really exist? When Peter Eisenman makes this perfect joint, where three axes come together in an inside and outside corner, it's something that you can draw or model but it is really hard to make in real life. Is that a lie? Should that be called out or is that just part of the craft of working with the limitations of materials and perception?

Ingraham: There is a necessity as part of the system of architecture for fiction. There's no reason why the corner can't be fictitious. The system can still digest it, refer to it, take photographs of it, and doctor photographs. It's absolutely necessary to have a cover-up.

Lavin: When Liz did the leaky Jean Nouvel exhibition at Fondation Cartier, it was funny in part because architects say the leak is not their fault. They make a distinction between plumbing and architecture. But as a practice, Diller Scofidio + Renfro is occupying the space between that gap which is what makes them different. We're all talking about The Shed and how amazing it is, but we're forgetting those first 15 years of your practice when everybody said about your work, "it's not architecture."

Diller: Our independent work is still independent work. But The Shed was an interesting problem. It was one thing to do a building on Hudson Yards, because we had to agree to do something on a developer's site. But in addition to that, we also agreed to do a developer building. At first, we said, "absolutely not." Then we thought about it and agreed because, as people pointed out, it was the only way to protect The Shed. It was basically an act of self-defense and opportunism.

Ultimately, everyone was using everyone and that's the reality of being an architect and getting something done. You can work autonomously and do things that are more controlled, or you can start to speak in different voices and to different audiences. You get things done while keeping your integrity. I think that's a very important skill.

Diller Scofidio + Renfro, Jet Lag, MASS MoCA, North Adams, MA, 1999

Aranda\ Lasch

Oyler Wu

01

04

06

08

09

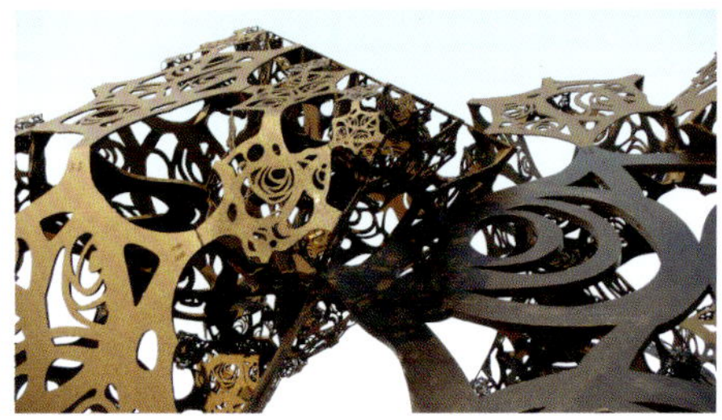

02

03

05

10

07

11

14

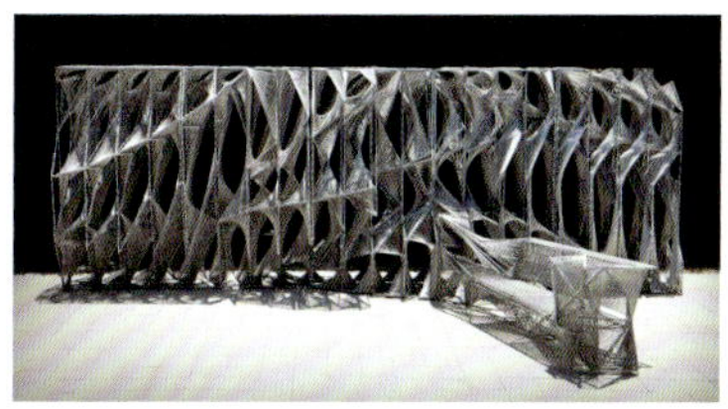

16

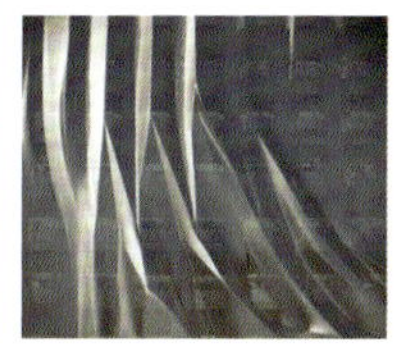

18

12

13

15

17

19

Introduction

DAVID ERDMAN

It's my pleasure to introduce our guests Jenny Wu and Dwayne Oyler of Oyler Wu Collaborative, and Benjamin Aranda of Aranda\Lasch, which he leads with Chris Lasch.

Both offices test the limits in mediums and continually examine what it means to practice architecture today. They stretch into territory that exceeds building. They work on product and furniture design, architecture, exhibition design, curating, and writing. The firms also use digital media and fabrication technologies in extensive ways.

Certainly, there are aesthetic and methodological differences between the two offices, but part of why we've asked them to present together as part of Pratt Sessions is their discourse on drawing. These practices use drawing in ways that might suggest that drawing is no longer what it used to be; that it's a new kind of medium. In this context, new doesn't necessarily mean that it has never been done before. Rather, it might be a different way of thinking about something that's quite established and rudimentary.

If the core definition of "the architect" is that we make drawings, I would characterize the work of these practitioners as drawing-building, where drawing and building are the same act. They become multi-dimensional mediums that happen at the same time.

One of the things that distinguishes the work of Aranda\Lasch within the discourse of drawing is its "foaminess." **01** Aggregated polyhedrons are often set side by side in tangential packing formations, **02** which gives the work a bubbly, molecular quality. In the context of drawing, it's difficult to tell what the typology is that describes this geometry. It's not subdivision of a surface or an aggregate "group-form," **03** but instead there's a subtle migration of the geometry and drawing type between scales, different approaches, and outputs. **04**

The work of Aranda\Lasch also shows a shifting dimensionality. It oscillates between 2D and 3D, and operates often in a 2.5-dimensional space. **05** The joint or virtual line between those geometries has a plastic quality with a range of dynamics—thick and thin, solid and void. **06**

From afar, many of their completed and proposed works look two-dimensional. **07** They almost seem to be super flat. There are moments in other projects that have a staccato quality. **08** As one moves into them, the line work starts to immerse you in three and four dimensions. **09** One starts to really feel the drawing more than one can see it. It is this simultaneity and shift of dimensions that can perhaps help us understand new ways of thinking about drawing. **10**

One could describe Oyler Wu Collaborative as "hyperbolic." I mean this in the geometrical sense rather than in the literary sense of the word. Dense line work is everywhere, immersing, entangling, obscuring both the event space and the form. **11** Projects seem to maximize the quantity and types of lines—profile lines, contour lines, etched and embossed lines. **12** **13**

While the line work has an intensity when you're close to it physically, the effect of these "drawings" from further away is one of softness. The work has a ghostly or aberrant quality. **14**

The more recent work has fissures where otherwise thick and heavy forms unleash torrents of line work. It's almost as if that line work is hemorrhaging out from the inside of the project. **15** **16** I would suggest that it's in these thick zones that the vitality of their work resides. Here, one no longer reads or analyzes drawing or line, but one starts to occupy the drawing/the line in a variety of ways. **17** **18** **19**

One could claim that drawing is the mainstream of architectural practice and discourse. In one of our early conversations about this evening's discussion, Ben Aranda pointed out that, as students, we were often told that architects don't "make buildings," but "draw them." This came from a much-used quote from Robin Evans and was the modus operandi in many educational institutions. But I'm not sure that what either of these firms is doing is part of the mainstream of disciplinary or professional understanding of drawings.

Certainly, Evans's reading of Daniel Libeskind's Chamber Works installation at the Architectural Association in 1983 was revelatory in terms of how we might begin to understand drawing. Evans's critique and praise of that show was that drawing itself started to become an experience; drawing was no longer just a representational medium, but it was the architecture itself.

Along the lines of a recent exhibition at the Parrish Museum, entitled *Image Building* (2018), we could understand drawing as a complementary form of building. That exhibition strategically shifted the ontological presumption that images

and photographers document real buildings. Instead, the show posited that buildings were designed for specific images that were not necessarily part of the actual human experience of the building. It implied that the vision of the camera, in fact, may have superseded the architectural design or imprinted the author's concept in some manner.

In the context of our discussion on New Architectural Mediums, we might suggest that what the camera was to the 20th century, the computer and artificial intelligence is to the 21st century. The experience of moving through a project by Oyler Wu or Aranda\Lasch is perhaps closer to the way one experiences a drawing in the computer or the way a computer might experience a drawing, and less similar to how a human would have experienced it on paper or in any other form of reality.

There's a sense of their projects being both welcoming and in some cases barely inhabitable. Projects by Oyler Wu and Aranda\Lasch are engaging the drawing as something that moves between dimensions of reality and perception simultaneously. The methods that drive their work, the breadth of formats they've tested and all the different means that they use, which range from very hands-on to very hands-off, have allowed our guests to expand their modes of practice in making. Something we will hear more about in the presentations to come.

Aranda\Lasch

NEW YORK, NY & TUCSON, AZ

To speak about drawing, I thought I'd be quite autobiographical and show you a book that really influenced me when I was in graduate school, called *Aberrations* by Jurgis Baltrušaitis from 1989.

The title comes from techniques of drawing anamorphoses or astrological aberrations. Baltrušaitis called these "depraved perspectives." What was so interesting to me about this book and its idea of drawing was that the "depraved perspectives" were where science and error or fiction would meet.

Baltrušaitis said, "The truth of metaphysics are the truth of the masks." Actually, the whole book is dedicated to the morphology of legends. Minerals depict living worlds and ruins, trees create cathedrals. Everything in these drawings has an immutable logic with strict tactical analysis, but there is a life to these forms.

In the book, Baltrušaitis also writes, "The life of forms depends not only on the site in which they actually exist, but also on that in which they are seen and recreate themselves."

This book and these drawings inspire me to think about how to use drawing to access not so much the world that we know, but the world we can invent.

As a practice, Aranda\Lasch went through about a decade of looking at a-periodic tiling. We looked at a three-dimensional Penrose tiling to see if we could find things that were impossible to find without the tool of drawing. In our Quasicabinet, for example, three-dimensional packing was only accessible using a fourth dimensional space.

Out of this interest in drawing and our interest in Baltrušaitis's book came our affinity toward history. We often use drawing to reimagine historical ideas, concepts, and objects.

Henri Labrouste did a drawing, entitled *Imaginary Reconstruction of an Ancient City* (undated). It's a drawing exercise of recreating an old structure based on its remaining ruins. What I find so amazing about this drawing process is that it's highly generative. The idea of having a drawing be about resuscitating or revisiting a historical moment is something that has existed in our practice from day one. In many of our projects we try and reread history. In 2007, we designed a chair that represents the year 1774—a year that the manganese crystal was discovered and the year that Louis XV died.

Related to an understanding of history as generative is a building that we completed in 2015 in Miami. We were asked to design a building for a luxury development called the Design District. We decided that we wanted to revisit Art Deco, which was a very important movement in Miami. But we wanted to revisit it with a certain rhythm and proportion. Rather than

Aranda\Lasch, Quasicabinet, 2007

Aranda\Lasch, Art Deco Project, Miami, FL, 2015

focusing on how to make Art Deco contemporary or buildable, we wanted to render the bright Miami sunlight. What the folds and the pleats of Art Deco offer you are ways of realizing how intense the sunlight is. The facade of our building is made of stone panels.

We've had a few other projects in Miami that have allowed us to explore ideas of material. We just completed a store for an Italian leather goods company, Valextra. The idea was to bring to Miami all the materials you would discover on the streets of Milan, such as on the facades of palazzos and the city's corners. We wanted to create a very intense material environment in which to display Valextra's goods.

Related to drawing is an ongoing collaboration with Terrol Dew Johnson, a Native American basket weaver. Part of the work was shown in 2016 at the Museum of Contemporary Art, Tucson. We call the objects "baskets" in the sense that they're vessels. They are designed and built with weavers from the Tohono O'odham Nation in southern Arizona. A lot of tribes have specific materials they like to use and their own way to weave and bind the materials. The Tohono O'odham typically use desert grass wrapped up with a sinew string.

A basket is essentially a coil that builds up a basket shape. Instead of coiling around itself, our idea was to coil in space. This allowed us to explore a traditional Native American basket, but with a new spatial logic in mind. Making these baskets has been a parallel trajectory in our practice and continues as we work on other projects.

All of this work can be described as a way of drawing. We call it "broken drawings," as they're fractal in nature. In fact, the word "fractal" means broken up. Benoit Mandelbrot coined the term in 1975 to describe a part that could be repeated to make up a more complex whole.

We've used that constraint throughout most of our projects. For instance, our Railing series of furniture objects are made of metal, coated with a silicone foam. They are all built with off-the-shelf parts—a configuration of 3-inch, 6-inch, 9-inch, 12-inch, and 18-inch sections of pre-bent pipe. This logic allows you to ensure that there's continuity.

Similarly, we have a long-standing collaboration with artist Matthew Richie. Essentially, we would design armatures and

Matthew would then draw on them. Our job was to make sure that, through the drawing, the piece would still stand or would be structural. These are bent drawings, loops that come back on themselves.

Also, a collaboration with Matthew is a work called The Morning Line, in which the drawing is the structure and the space. It's a three-dimensional drawing but in the way that it's built, the units are all the same. In this way, you can also describe it as a one-dimensional construction, where the only thing you need to know is the rotation of the piece in space.

The last project I would like to present is Another Circle, which was our installation in Columbus, Indiana. It's a big circle made of pieces of limestone, which form spaces that you can sit or picnic on. Indiana is covered with limestone. We visited a few local mills and realized that they throw out a lot of material. We asked a mill in Bloomington, called Bybee Stone, if we could use their offcuts. They agreed, so we needed no material budget for the installation. Instead, the project became about how you organize refuse: while you can't control the exact look of it, you can control the placement.

We organized points in space so that they would create a program. Those points were translated into GPS coordinates. This mapping became the drawing, which was loaded into an app. We worked with amazing contractors, the Taylor Brothers, who were able to build the installation using their phones. They didn't use any traditional construction equipment—no tape measure, string, levels, or power tools. The only thing they had was their phones and a GPS emitter that would create a more accurate reading than you can get from a GPS satellite.

We were able to get an accuracy within an inch. The construction workers would walk around, follow the GPS points on the map, and they would place the stone in that location. When they hit a point, the app would tell them how high to build or whether a piece of stone should be at an angle or not.

Aranda\Lasch, Valextra Bal Harbour Store, Miami, FL, 2018

Aranda\Lasch, Railing series, 2015

From that information, we were able to create different kinds of furniture settings at different heights.

We were quite interested in letting go of control to allow the construction team to come up with their own ideas of what they should build. It possibly points towards a way of building where we can relinquish some control but still be the authors of the project from a conceptual sense.

Aranda\Lasch with Matthew Ritchie, The Morning Line, Seville, Spain, 2008

Aranda\Lasch, Another Circle, Columbus, IN, 2018

Oyler Wu Collaborative

LOS ANGELES, CA

Our office is based in Los Angeles, which has been an important part of the architects that we've become. We were on the East Coast for a long time, but when we went to LA, we found an incredible convergence of things that we hadn't anticipated. There is an incredible architecture culture and our colleagues are competitive in the most productive way. There's also a can-do, build-it-in-your-backyard attitude that has been very helpful in the way we think about how to produce work.

We work at all scales. We recently completed a 16-story building in Taipei, but we've also been involved with installations, and designing furniture, jewelry, and industrial design objects. We're always very conscious about there being a dialogue between the smaller things that we're doing and the larger things. We rarely go into the design of a smaller element without thinking how it's going to come to bear on the larger projects.

The way we work is probably about as diverse as the scale of our projects. We grew up at a time when we were transitioning from drawing by hand to working digitally. Without consciously doing so, we've held on to everything that came along the way, including hand drawing. Model building has always been an important part of the office. Making is an immediate way of

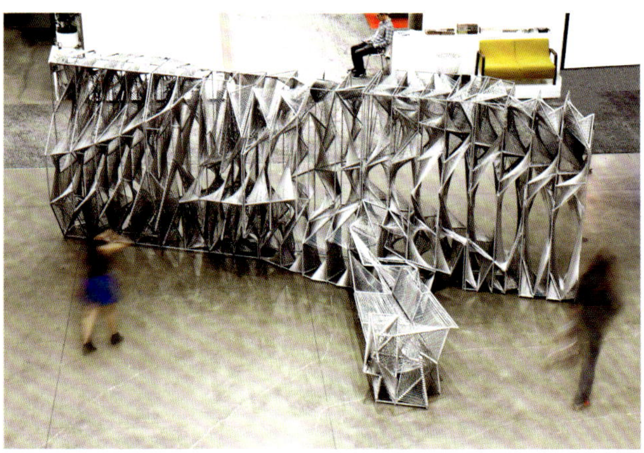

Oyler Wu Collaborative, Screenplay, SFMOMA, San Francisco, CA, 2012

imagining things and conceiving of ideas.

For a project like Screenplay, which we completed in 2012, once the initial form was figured out, it came down to the details of the way that the rope was knotted. No end of a rope was ever shown. We built model after model in order to figure out those details.

We've built a lot of our installations ourselves. We started out doing these projects out of necessity. We couldn't afford to have built what we were proposing. We thought we would grow out of that quickly; that clients would come along with enormous budgets and they'd pay for fabrication.

Of course, that didn't happen as quickly as we thought it would. But as we did start to work with clients who could pay for the construction of our designs, we made a conscious effort to continue fabricating ourselves. We realized that with every project, those types of projects were bringing something new to the office. At the very least, they kept us evolving because we would get bored building the same kind of work repeatedly.

Over the last 10 years, we've worked with the idea of line, surface, and volume as a way of developing the work. For several years leading up to that moment, we had been doing a lot of drawings. Common issues of density and depth were reoccurring. We were thinking about what are the qualities that are inherent to line, things that don't happen if you're working with surface or volume. For example, foreground and background, and the instantaneous shift of focus between one and the other. While there's occasionally a focal point, you can use the ambiguity created by issues of line weight to further enhance the idea of moving back and forth between foreground and background.

Around this time, we did four projects with bent aluminum tube. In these projects, we started to introduce curvature as a way to solve the problem of complexity. Prior to these projects, we were working with cut joints. We were welding them, grinding them back clean, and polishing them to make smooth joints. But as we began proposing projects that had too many of those joints, we introduced curves. Working with a radial draw bender, we could achieve a greater complexity. It opened up the reading of the work to become a continuous field of bent aluminum moving through space.

After these installations, we moved into projects that were even more intensely line-based. They were less structural and more about pattern recognition and the perception of 2D versus 3D.

Alongside each of these line-based projects, we were starting to work on projects that were bigger and that had a more robust set of requirements, as most architecture does. We started to think about issues like surface. How do we keep the

Oyler Wu Collaborative, Lineworks, Ongoing Series

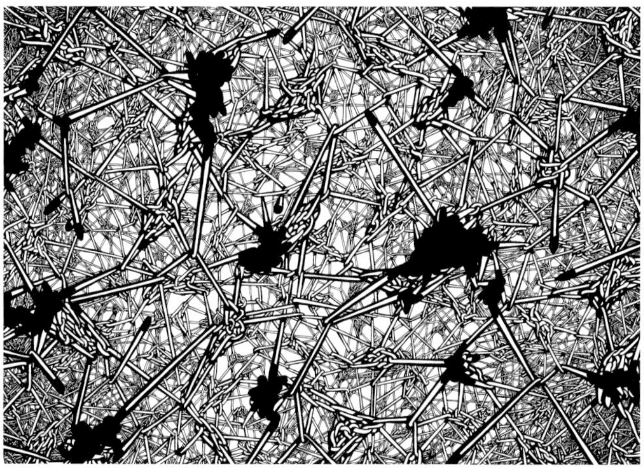

Oyler Wu Collaborative, Lineworks, Ongoing Series

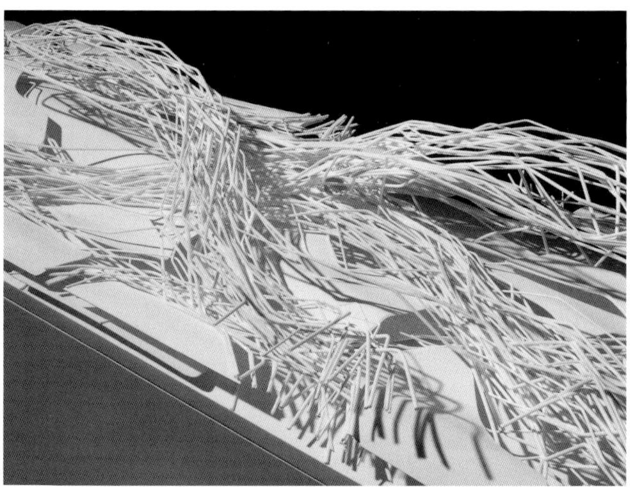

Oyler Wu Collaborative, Trajectories, Los Angeles, CA, 2008

rain out? However, in introducing surface we specifically didn't want to abandon line. We felt like we had built up a catalog of ideas around line that could easily just be swept away. The resulting projects always had a loose fit relationship between the surfaces and lines. At times, lines would run along the edge of a surface. Other times, they would be offset or shifted in order to remain autonomous.

We started looking at models and evaluating them in much the same way we were examining the earlier drawings. We asked ourselves whether we could mine the models for information or principles to guide us. We were insistent on a three-dimensionality so that the line can move in and out of the surface. Our Hi Res Low Rise proposal is an example when you see the line and surface dialogue. The brief was for the renovation of a building with a skin to cut down on solar gain. In our proposal, the majority of the building had a simple, tight-fit framework of aluminum perforation. But there was a restaurant on the ground floor, where this geometric piece came down and began to peel away from the geometry of the line work. Here, the line work becomes a more autonomous element.

About five years ago, we started working in Asia. At that point, we were mostly working on line-based installations. A few developers suggested that we might size up some of these ideas to the scale of a building. We worked through many iterations of what a high-rise building should be. Finally, we convinced a developer that we were exactly who they wanted and needed. The problem with many projects in Asia is that the exact plan is already established, and as an architect you get only a small envelope in which to work. For the Monarch in Taipei, we tried to make it feel volumetric. We wrapped the corners of the building with expanded mesh panels. Aluminum line pieces start to change the design of the facade.

Like Aranda\Lasch, we designed an installation in Columbus, Indiana. Each installation was paired with an existing local work by a master architect. We were given a site next to the former Irwin Union Bank, designed by Eero Saarinen. It was a challenging project for us in that we were not only trying to understand how we might be able to contribute to this community but also thinking about how we might think about Saarinen in this context and about our work in the context of Saarinen.

In Saarinen's building, three canopies served the drive-through bank tellers. We used those as a starting point and wrapped L-shaped walls with inlay of either a framed object or a framed wall with a solid object embedded.

We produced very elaborate drawings to determine how we might pack the constructed pieces of this installation into two semi-trucks to be transported to Columbus. One of the

things that we've been interested in for a long time is trying to figure out how to elevate the role of the detailed drawing. Most often, drawing is a space of speculation. But there's one kind of drawing that doesn't do that—the construction drawing. In fact, its intention is to eliminate as much speculation as possible.

We have been interested in producing construction and somehow elevate their status to presentation drawing. They can have the same dense qualities that presentation drawings might have. They can have an order to them, but one that's ambiguous and difficult to find. It takes a level of direct engagement to understand the relationship between parts.

Oyler Wu Collaborative, Hi Res Low Rise, Los Angeles, CA, 2011

Oyler Wu Collaborative, Monarch, Taipei, Taiwan, 2017

Oyler Wu Collaborative, The Exchange, Columbus, IN, 2017

Oyler Wu Collaborative, The Exchange, Columbus, IN, 2017

Conversation

ARANDA\LASCH AND OYLER WU COLLABORATIVE

David Erdman: Marshall McLuhan's understanding of a medium is that it's somehow extended from the body. With drawing there's an intermediate tool like a pencil between the mind and the result on paper, but it has always been a clear form of extension. With the digital age that extension rapidly accelerated.

As a result, there was a sense of anxiety within architectural discourse about a potential for over-extension; a worry that the discipline might lose the ability to draw. Certainly, you hear conflicting messages that are coming out of juries today. On one hand, why are we talking about drawing? We don't really need it from a technological perspective. At the same time, you hear professors saying students don't know how to draw. Is there a crisis of drawing in the discipline?

Benjamin Aranda: I'd suggest changing one word in the Robin Evans quote mentioned earlier, which said that architects don't make buildings, architects make drawings of buildings. I would argue that architects don't make buildings, architects make *instructions* for buildings. For us, the idea of producing instructions encompasses drawings, but there are media that have really opened up the idea for architects to produce buildings beyond having to delineate them. We can script them. We can automate them.

Certainly, we're moving into an exciting territory with machine learning and using feedback. It's a highly McLuhan-esque phenomena. My optimism makes me believe that architects are trained in all these things. We're trained not just to draw, but to be sensitive to the things you need to instruct construction. That doesn't have to be 2D anymore. What I was trying to get at with my presentation was the idea that you could run through various forms of dimensions from 1D to more than 3D. It really is about how you encapsulate the ability to instruct or to codify construction.

Dwayne Oyler: I try not to say that students can't draw anymore. I have probably said that a couple times in the past but I've meant something different. I mean they can't speculate, because I typically would use the drawing as a means of speculating. Sometimes students don't have a mechanism for imagining, communicating that imagination, and then allowing it to evolve as pencil or pen is on paper.

Erdman: Traditionally, the way I've understood it is that because a drawing is much less extended from the physical body and it can't be made so instantaneously, your mind can develop an imaginary counterpart to it. When it's instantaneous and you press a button and it comes out, there's skepticism about human intelligence, being able to engage in the same way that you do when it's less extended.

Oyler: I agree that it's not as immediate. But on the other hand, there was an immediacy to the hand, because it put what is in your mind right there in front of you. In a way, it takes more time working digitally.

The other thing I mean when I say students can't draw, is that students can't see. At the end of the day, people who draw well usually do so because they can see well. They've learned to look at something, produce an image in their head that was close enough to their memory that when they put it on a piece of paper, they know whether the pen or the pencil should go right or left. In our office we've tried to collapse drawing from the moment of speculation to the time it is constructed so that they're as close together as they can be.

Erdman: What I find exciting about both of your work is that it suggests a very different kind of medium than the conventional understanding of drawing. It does require seeing and some sense of interpretation, but it's probably more cyborg-like or slightly more post-human. It no longer defines creativity and the act of drawing as necessarily starting with the human. Therefore, it also doesn't assume that you're losing anything because you're not the one making it.

Jenny Wu: To return to the Robin Evans quote, I really like the collapse of drawing and architecture into one. I think this extends into this conversation about us being kind of cyborgian. In fact, at the end of the day, there are a lot of things that we don't draw because we know we'll have to make them ourselves. If we know we cannot bend this curve, we don't draw this curve. There is a buildup of knowledge of how far we can push an assembly of material. We put all that knowledge together and then push it into architecture. That's where I feel like architects are synthesizing knowledge, technique, and drawing to create something that's cyborgian.

Aranda: There's an important element of discovery that happens through drawing that's almost in opposition or

in resistance to this conversation of progress. The reason I started my presentation with the drawings from *Aberrations* is that error or accident and these "depraved moments" are important disciplinary mechanisms. They actually exist and crop up repeatedly as ways that the discipline as a whole learns to reinvent itself. Paul Virilio said that every technology is matched by an accident. It's important not to forget that we need mechanisms in the discipline that force us to resist the seduction of technology.

Erdman: There's a counter-movement to it amongst the current generation of students. Do you see that as a productive, distinctive claim?

Aranda: Yes, it's almost a natural process that at the edge of things. If you look at disciplines as natural processes, at the very edge there's a decomposition where matter unfolds much more unpredictably when it's encountered with something different from itself. I think the discipline is like that as well. Right at the

From left to right: David Erdman, Benjamin Aranda, Jenny Wu, and Dwayne Oyler in conversation at Pratt Sessions 10.

edge are these unknown areas. In the academies and associated practices, we've taken upon ourselves as architects that want to discover that edge. Part of that edge is pursuing technique at its highest caliber. I think it's also pursuing moments of error, glitch, accident, resistance. Looking for ways to ruin it, because without that, there's no way forward. Progress on its own is not going to win.

Erdman: Well, if you watch *Westworld*, you'd say that just means it's not human. Maybe that is still a thirst for it to have a humane quality. We want it to have errors, because we see that blemish. There's an inordinate amount of literature about that. That's just part of the human condition—we fuck everything up. Once it doesn't have that in it, then it can't be us and we're extinct.

Oyler: Ben, you said resist, but I think what makes your work great is that you fully embrace it, but resist it to a certain extent. The best work on the edge recognizes that it comes with a certain kind of identity and quality that is instantly recognizable as missing something. I've never thought of whether it's human error. It's not produced using automated processes, for example. We've always been very skeptical of drawings that are the result of an automated process. We became architects largely because we wanted to make deliberate decisions.

Aranda: Yeah, I would say that the "crisis in drawing" is probably indicative of a wider crisis in determinism or in techniques that try to locate something very specifically. We live in an age when the nuances are very important. Collectively, we're going through a very difficult time right now in terms of politics and social media. A lot of technology itself is on the chopping board. Facebook, Amazon, Netflix, and Google are now all being subpoenaed and having to sit before congressional committees to tell us why things are not working. Why is society breaking down? Why are we having all these problems when this was supposed to be the solution?

These are the moments to which Virilio referred, where it's the glitches that are as revealing as the technology itself. As architects, we're complicit in that. I think we need to carry with us as practitioners a hint of skepticism. Yes, we have to be absolutely rigorous and we have to be as sophisticated in our techniques as possible. But when we travel with those techniques, we also travel with other things. We carry the understanding that they only go so far. That's really where it comes to a question of ethics. It's not something that we can teach. We can only go so far. The generation that's becoming architects now, with all of these crises of technique: you're coming into a world where you have to step up and show us the way forward.

Sanford Kwinter, in the audience: I just want to push you all one more step. Many people in the room remember when CDs first appeared. Everybody was totally excited by them; we had a whole new mobile way of having music. Some snobs said, "No, I can hear the difference," but everyone thought that was absolutely preposterous. Here we are, some 25 years later, and almost nobody would have difficulty distinguishing the differences in the sound of an analog signal and a CD.

The general capacity for discernment has got us to a place where, in fact, we simply can perceive what we couldn't perceive all those years ago. Now, it's irrefutable that the digital milieu speaks incredibly powerful in your work. I just want to see if you can respond to this as if it mattered to make a statement about how your education and how those stages in the development of your methodologies may now need to change or to begin to focus on, you might say, everything that belongs to, as Virilio would say, the opposite ethos.

Aranda: I'll be very honest: I see us as a practice in transition and transformation. We're actively trying to not do things that we did before. The Columbus, Indiana stone project was a real challenge for us to build in as discreet a way as we always wanted to build, but to relinquish control to the people building it and to the material. Being open to change, to new things, and to reinvention is a hot topic in the office. There was a real learning curve that came out of those early years. I think we still have a lot to learn. To me, it's more about how do you confront change. How do you evolve as a practice?

Kwinter: Those are all the metaphors of life.

Aranda: Yeah, that's the fun part about having a body of work. It's a pleasure to look back at ten years of work to see the consistencies, but also to see the breakdowns. We're fortunate enough to be in a position where with new projects, we can ask if we want to reset the course.

Oyler: Yeah, we should absolutely be asking ourselves, "have we set a course that we can't veer off of?" If we have, that's a huge problem, because we don't know what's to come.

Erdman: I think both practices are great examples of evolving out of the digital turn. There are very material qualities that can't be predictable to whatever instruction you think you're giving the material. There's an intelligence to the material

that's imprinting itself on the practices as they mature, and that's evolving the way that you're drawing and thinking. When considering human intelligence and material intelligence, there is probably a third intelligence we need to talk about now. Instead of them being necessarily antagonistic or aggrandizing one another, that it might be more about how you get those three things to have proximity or veer off from one another. Computational intelligence will certainly be part of that in the 21st century as artificial intelligence grows and becomes another being.

Overview

Pratt
GAUD
PS08
PITA + BLOOM
PITA & BLOOM
LOS ANGELES
+
YOUNG + AYATA
YOUNG & AYATA
NEW YORK
03.01.18
THURSDAY 6PM
HIGGINS HALL AUDITORIUM
POP UP EXHIBITION
PHILIPP SCHAERER & LESLIE WAYNE
PRATT SESSIONS 08
NEW ARCHITECTURAL MEDIUMS

Pratt
GAUD
PS09
LIZ DILLER
DILLER SCOFIDIO + RENFRO
NEW YORK
+
SYLVIA LAVIN
UCLA
LOS ANGELES
CATHERINE INGRAHAM
MODERATOR
04.05.18
THURSDAY 6PM
HIGGINS HALL AUDITORIUM
POP UP EXHIBITION
FIONA CONNOR
THOMAS DEMAND
PRATT SESSIONS 09
NEW ARCHITECTURAL MEDIUMS
PHOTO CREDIT: Diller Scofidio + Renfro

PHOTO CREDIT: ARANDA LASCH ARCHITECTS
Pratt
GAUD
PS10
ARANDA
BENJAMIN ARANDA
ARANDA-LASCH ARCHITECTS
NEW YORK
+
OYLER + WU
DWAYNE OYLER + JENNY WU
OYLER WU COLLABORATIVE
LOS ANGELES
09.20.18
THURSDAY 6PM
HIGGINS HALL AUDITORIUM
POP UP EXHIBITION
TO BE ANNOUNCED
PRATT SESSIONS 10
NEW ARCHITECTURAL MEDIUMS

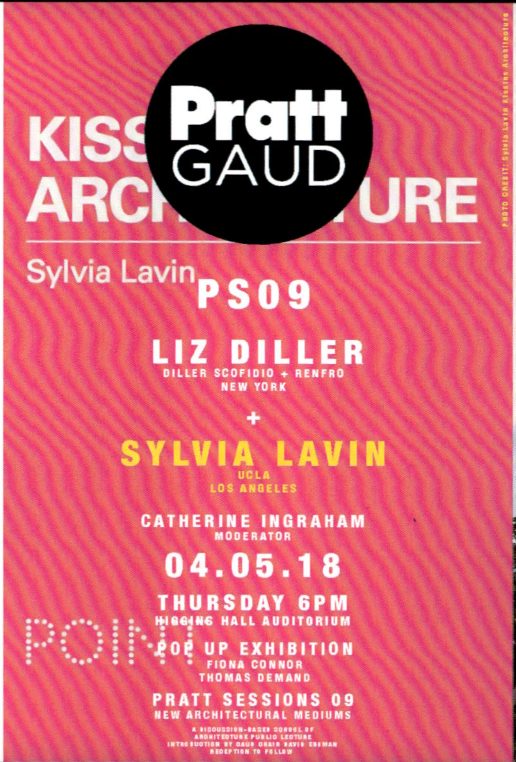

PHOTO CREDIT: Sylvia Lavin Kissing Architecture

Dean's Note

TOM HANRAHAN
DEAN OF THE SCHOOL OF ARCHITECTURE

Now in its second year, *Pratt Sessions* is a new publication developed by the Graduate Architecture and Urban Design programs in Pratt Institute's School of Architecture. The school has long been host to a series of innovative publications that not only introduced readers to emerging ideas in architecture and design but presented them in new and experimental forms. Over three decades the *Pratt Journal*, *In Process,* and *TARP* have expanded the boundaries of theoretical, visual, and topical design journals. *Pratt Sessions* joins this distinctive group with its own inventive format, and rich array of completed work and theoretical speculations by some of the most important architects and designers practicing today.

Each section of *Pratt Sessions* is a transcribed public conversation between paired designers and architects, augmented by examples of their work and observations and questions by moderator and chair of Graduate Architecture and Urban Design David Erdman. The results are provocative and unexpected and provide insights into architecture and design that are not always revealed in more traditional lecture formats. Some of these conversations demonstrate broad agreement on critical ideas in design, while others illustrate the unique differences in approach and thinking from this exceptionally talented group of contributors. All of them touch on the most important issues affecting the design of spaces, buildings and cities today. Together they illustrate the remarkable range and complexity of thought that can be found in today's design world.

M6

Introduction

DAVID ERDMAN
CHAIRPERSON, ASSOCIATE PROFESSOR
GRADUATE ARCHITECTURE + URBAN DESIGN

In surfing, a "session" is a period in which you make something out of nothing. A moment of precision, in which one reads, galvanizes, exploits, and interacts with a consortium of forces. It is as euphoric as it is fleeting, as mysterious as it is understood. Surfers spend their lives craving a good session. The musical equivalent is not so different. Often unpaid, informal gatherings harnessing live performance or improvised recording, one could argue that a good musical session (if witnessed or documented) is the engine behind a musician's growth. Be it musician to musician, human to aquatic medium, or architect to architect, the spirit of the Pratt Sessions is to debate, question and discuss matters on the periphery and core of our discipline. To capture a fleeting moment with some precision and allow it to alter, shift, and transform dynamically.

The Pratt Sessions are conceived as a distributed symposium focused on two parallel research subjects we are currently examining in the Graduate Architecture and Urban Design programs; Architectural Mediums and Contexts. Like a surfing session, these sessions are meant to galvanize something out of subtle aberrations, to read the surface closely, to gain an understanding of its depths, and to have an improvisational one-off quality; each discussion being different and having to negotiate the particularities of that specific event and its participants.

Bringing together pairings of designers and thinkers, one of whom is regional and the other non-regional (predominately from New York City and Los Angeles), the sessions curb stereotypes and assumptions about the thermohaline circulation of architecture discourse; I am here borrowing heavily from surfology, using the term for oceanic swells and current flows as an analogy for the formation of the Kittler-like discourse networks in architecture. The thermohaline circulation of the sessions is an analogy to the redistributing those networks, and their associate cultural/communal bi-products for the GAUD, School of Architecture, Pratt, national and international communities.

Like the oceanographic science of predicting current flows and understanding their engrained patterns, the circuitry of architecture discourse has been in an East to Westward flow in North America since its instantiation in the late 19th and early 20th century, and has been reinscribed and stabilized through the mid- and late 20th century. One could chart this thermohaline flow in higher education as moving from Ivy to Prairie to the Wild Wild West. The intellectual culture of architecture and requisite institutions thus re-inscribe Manifest Destiny often with a pejorative set of associated overtones: the East is where you think about it and the West is where you just do it! Laid back versus uptight, sunny versus cloudy, the climatological and cultural overtones continued to divide East and West Coast cultures and discourse networks until the late 20th century when they began to reverse.

The mechanics of these established modalities of thinking, intellectual culture, and lifestyle are shifting. We feel this acutely here at Pratt—located in a primary cultural hub in Brooklyn. Back flows, ebbs, and reversals of discourse and influence can be seen across the East Coast, even seeping back into Europe where West is now influencing East. Just look at how many teachers, deans, and chairs on the East Coast are former West Coast faculty and vice versa. The curatorial approach of the sessions was to both recognize the established and historical circuitry of discourse while trying to entangle and identify its reversals and ambiguities. The sessions became an immediate and swift way to gauge the degree to which those stereotypes reassert themselves and measure where they fall apart; using the subjects of mediums and contexts as an instigator to fuel the fire.

The participants in the sessions are curated as much for their similarities as they are for their differences. They are asked to focus presentations on the given subject as a means of enriching a precise discourse and to foster student discussion; a central factor in the origins of the series. The discussions have extended for hours after presentations completed and are all followed by continued debate and discussion during the reception and Pop-Up Exhibition, including work from two artists the participants have nominated. The artist inclusions often further enriched the discourse and potential affiliations with subjects and other discourse networks—bearing the fruits of being housed within an art, architecture, and design institute such as Pratt.

My job as the introducer of these events has been not so much to laud my esteemed colleagues nor account for their work in a manner accurate to either their writing or others' writings about their work. Instead it has been to give their work a narrow reading in relation to the theme at hand. I see my introductions, included here with the presentations and conversations, as one part warm up band—priming the arena for the main act—and one part having a productively oblique relationship to what the presenters may or may not show, which was often not known in advance.

This second volume of Pratt Sessions collects six sessions, three focused on each subject, involving seventeen participants; including moderators, spanning one year. Among them are six leading female thinkers and designers, six participants from the west coast and one from the mid-west. While each section is presented chronologically within the two subjects, they are not in the exact order in which they occurred over the course of the year. The subjects and lectures were "interdigitated," allowing for a switching from one subject to the other and to unfold over the semester and year. This configuration produces a rich texture of thinking, a range of opinions, and a productively "selective amnesia" about the subjects at hand. A distinct advantage to distributing a symposium and/or discussion with this type of structure is its capacity for inclusivity, diversity, as well as unanticipated redundancies, overlaps, and bifurcations. The book design is multi-axial in response, using different page orientations—front, back, portrait, and landscape—to coalesce. This was the graphic counterpart to infusing the book with productive yet coarse mixtures of readings with the hope that one might flip between all three sections, and discover this introduction, for example, well after reading other portions of the book. The middle section of this volume collects the proper "front" of the book; now dislocated to the center and in a different page orientation. It gathers introductory material, including an essay by Sanford Kwinter, introduction by former Dean Tom Hanrahan, and the Pop-Up Exhibition artists and artworks. The two sessions sections are mirrored, forming a palindromic structure that allows for reading in two directions. They include edited versions of the introductions I delivered as well as the edited versions of the participants' presentations and the conversations that followed. The book is designed to enable the reader to experience and navigate multiple sessions, browsing and "surfing" between subjects, introductions, and presentations.

This second collection, like the first, owes a great deal to its participants who willingly dove into somewhat unpredictable territory. It is my opinion that it is within this zone of the session that we are the most aware, attentive, and engaged. It is when those flows switch and reverse, open up counterintuitive readings and understandings that one might find a trajectory through the discourse valuable to his or her own work, thinking, or studies.

Terroir and Truth

SANFORD KWINTER

As the great neurologist Kurt Goldstein taught, "there is simply greater revelation in pathological phenomena." What he was signaling is that the operating system of any organism or ecology would not normally be visible under standard conditions of functioning—its logic would be embedded and largely masked by the explicit, more spectacular display of behaviors and forms.

To gain access to the operations that govern it, to the intelligence that controls the modes of expression, one needs an obstacle, a gap, a resistance, or an interruption of preset routines that causes the system to actively innovate and adapt before one's observing attention. It is through and within these improvisatory performances that deeper understanding becomes possible.

At no time in the history of our own discipline have the motivations behind design work become so cryptic and oblique, like a screen or fog that protects the stylish and growing fecklessness of contemporary pedagogy and practice. Given that so many institutions and practices have not only abandoned the checks-and-balances regimens of "theory" but now often affect explicitly and purposely to renounce it, the wider need for insight and understanding is being pursued by other means. Among these are the growing popularity of the "dyad lecture" in which two related practices and worldviews are brought into relation to generate a differential—no matter small or large—in whose gap the logics of commitment can more clearly be heard and seen. Pratt has commissioned now three year-long sets of such dyadic engagements and it has not shied away from amplifying the discords, controversies, but also the splendors and bankruptcies that such rap battles can implicitly expose.

What has been fascinating is that the revelatory "rifts" do not necessarily, or only, appear within or among the paired presenters (whose generational commonality is almost always preserved), but tellingly between the fulsome consensus the twinned speakers sometimes display and the discrepancy their collective affirmation can generate against a wider historical view or broader awareness of alternative cosmopolitan practice.

What is rich and salvational about such innocent and genuinely collegial dyadic performances is that they generate the function of dissent by their very nature and structure (although sometimes, to be sure, the audience has to call it out) without needing to rely, as in the past, on the courage, principled attitudes, or critical-philosophical labor of the individual actors in question. Pathological revelation is a rich byproduct of these "tender agonisms."

These are then, at their best and most rewarding, forensic practices. But forensics need not only be seen as forms of discovery to elucidate pernicious realities but rather as a methodology for penetrating the veil of gross appearances to achieve greater access to the nuances, admixtures, and creative operations of molecular (meaning underlying, composing) forces, properties, and interactions.

In the world of wine culture, and later across the entire landscape of culinary practice from foraging, farming, mise-en-place, preparation, transformation, expression, presentation, and so on, the concept of "terroir" expresses the infinity of connections that connect what appears on the plate and is delivered to the palate to the specific universe of historical and material conditions in which it was formed. Terroir refers to the infinitely subtle variations of expression that can be extracted

continuously from the earth, climate, culture, and even mindsets present in the ecology that developed and harbored them within the raw products from which they are subsequently refined. In this sense all form and substance is seen as generated by, and inextricably linked to, combinatory relationships that are always specific and timely and subject to capture and elucidation.

The new and cryptic conditions of today's design milieus are ever-more-importantly subject to these same probing operations of exploration, experiment, and interrogation. At no time in recent history have the logical forces that produce design propositions been so obscure in their philosophical foundations or relations to the operations of their own history. Yet every project and practice constitutes the expression of a veiled and mysterious logic or intelligence that may or may not be sound or authentic but which nonetheless represents the full truth or lie of creative formal practice. Every generation of practitioner selects and extracts features and properties from its educational milieu and historical experience and converts these into formal arguments and "facts." To listen and to watch these demonstrations is no different than to open one's sensibilities to the wonders and richesses of material culture as one does at the chef's table or sommelier's cave.

But the question is where and when the cooking and consumption procedures are made to take place, and who takes on the responsibility of concern for the properties of the terroir that lies operational within. Who takes responsibility for the forces that make and shape us? If no longer the architect-at-her/his-table or screen then it must be to those of us who listen, watch, combust, and consume, we who provide the intellectual framework of architectural consumption—who stage and "set up" the pathologies so that they may become more accessible to those who watch than to those who present.

This attitude may be the next necessary phase of architectural—and perhaps all other—education, and it is one that is being increasingly integrated into our pedagogy at Pratt.

Florencia Pita & Jackilin Hah Bloom

Florencia Pita is the principal of the Los Angeles-based design office Florencia Pita & Co., a creative platform dedicated to exploring architecture's multiple capacities, from the elements of the domestic environment to the objects of the urban landscape. Since 2005, she has developed projects in a wide variety of mediums and scales, from product design and exhibition design to building design and landscape design. The driving ideas behind her projects are based on her relentless use of color in architecture and the search of novel and yet familiar forms. Pita graduated in 1998 from the National University of Rosario, Argentina, School of Architecture, with licensure. In 1999 she was awarded the 2000 Fulbright-Fondo Nacional de las Artes Scholarship to pursue studies at Columbia University, where she received her MSAAD, Master's Degree in 2001. Florencia holds a full-time design faculty position and is the current graduate thesis coordinator at SCI-Arc, she also holds a visiting professorship appointment at the University of Pennsylvania's PennDesign Department and Princeton University's School of Architecture. In 2018 she was a Louis I. Kahn visiting assistant professor of Architectural Design at Yale School of Architecture. Her projects have been exhibited in major Institutions worldwide, and her work is part of several museum collections, such as MoMA, MAK Vienna, the Art Institute of Chicago, and UMMA Museum, among others. At the same time her work has been featured in numerous publications such as *Art Papers*, *Log* (in 2009 Pita was the co-editor of Log 17), and *Architecture Record*.

Jackilin Hah Bloom is an architectural designer and educator based in Los Angeles. She is the principal of Jackilin Hah Bloom Studio (JHB Studio) and a full-time faculty member at SCI-Arc. She received a Master of Architecture degree from UCLA in 2010 and a Bachelor of Architecture degree from USC in 1993. She worked for Greg Lynn for 10 years and for Daly Genik Architects for five years. From 2011-2018, Jackilin collaborated with Florencia Pita on many research-based projects, which have been recognized by numerous publications, exhibitions, and awards, most notably the U.S. Pavilion's exhibit, *The Architectural Imagination* at the 2016 Venice Architecture Biennale, and as finalists for the MoMA PS1 Young Architects Program. Recently, one of their studies on social housing in Mexico was selected as part of a collection of prototype homes to be constructed in Apan, Mexico by early 2019. Jackilin's teaching appointments include the schools of architecture at Princeton University, Yale University, Ohio State University, and Syracuse University. At SCI-Arc she teaches both undergraduate and graduate design studios, and visual studies seminars and has been a coordinator of the second-year core program.

Young & Ayata

Young & Ayata formed a partnership in New York in 2008 to explore the conceptual and aesthetic possibilities of architecture and urbanism. The practice is dedicated to both built commissions and experimental research. The practice views the reality of contemporary building as a provocation for architectural form, material, and technology. In following these trajectories, it is necessary to understand architecture in its historical processes. Both principals teach and view the educational experience as crucial to the continual development of architectural ideas.

Young & Ayata are the recipients of the 2016 Design Vanguard Award from *Architectural Record*. The Apartment building DL-310 designed in collaboration with Michan Architecture received the 2019 Progressive Architecture Award from *Architect Magazine*. In 2015, they were one of two first prize winners in the international competition for the New Bauhaus Museum in Dessau, Germany. They were finalists in the 2015 MoMA YAP Program in Istanbul, Turkey. In 2014, the partners were the recipients of the Young Architects Prize from the Architectural League of New York, and their entry in the open international competition for the Dalseong Citizen's Gymnasium in South Korea received an honorable mention. A manifesto titled, *The Estranged Object: Realism in Art and Architecture*, written by Michael Young with the projects of Young & Ayata was published in the Spring of 2015 by the Graham Foundation. Recently, the firm's work was exhibited at the Museum of Modern Art, the Istanbul Modern, the Graham Foundation, SCI-Arc, and Princeton University.

Elizabeth Diller is a founding partner of Diller Scofidio + Renfro (DS+R) an interdisciplinary design studio based in New York. Liz's cross-genre work has been distinguished with TIME's "100 Most Influential People" list and the first MacArthur Foundation fellowship awarded in the field of architecture. DS+R completed two of the largest architecture and planning initiatives in New York City's recent history: the adaptive reuse of an obsolete, industrial rail infrastructure into the High Line, a 1.5 mile-long public park, and the transformation of Lincoln Center for the Performing Arts' half-century-old campus.

In addition, she has led two cultural works significant to New York: The Shed—the first multi-arts center designed to commission, produce, and present all types of performing arts, visual arts, and popular culture—and the expansion of MoMA. Liz also created, directed, and produced The Mile-Long Opera, an immersive choral work featuring 1,000 singers staged on the High Line.

Most recently, DS+R was selected to design the London Centre for Music and a new Collection and Research Centre for the V&A in London's Olympic Park. Liz is a professor of Architecture at Princeton University.

Elizabeth Diller

Sylvia Lavin

Sylvia Lavin is a historian, critic, and curator of architecture and design. She received her Ph.D. from Columbia University in 1990 and the MIT Press published her first books *Quatremère de Quincy and the Invention of a Modern Language of Architecture* and *Form Follows Libido: Architecture and Richard Neutra in a Psychoanalytic Culture* in 1992 and 2005. Her most recent books include, *Kissing Architecture*, published by Princeton University Press in 2011 and *Flash in the Pan*, an AA publication. Her exhibitions include *Architecture Itself and Other Postmodernist Myths* (CCA 2018), *Super Models* (Chicago Architecture Biennial 2016), and *Everything Loose Will Land, Art and Architecture in LA in the 1970s* (The MAK/Schindler House, The Graham Foundation, and Yale School of Architecture 2013-14).

She is professor of architecture at Princeton University and was director of the Critical Studies program in the Department of Architecture and Urban Design at UCLA, where she was chairperson from 1996 to 2006.

Aranda\Lasch is a New York and Tucson-based design studio, established by Benjamin Aranda and Chris Lasch, designing buildings, installations, and furniture. Recognition includes the United States Artists Award, Young Architects Award, Design Vanguard Award, AD Innovators, and the Architectural League Emerging Voices Award.

Their early projects are the subject of the books *Tooling* and more recently *Trace Elements*.

Aranda\Lasch has exhibited internationally in galleries, museums, design fairs, and biennials. Their work is part of the permanent collection of the MoMA in New York. Benjamin currently teaches at the Cooper Union in New York.

Aranda\Lasch

Oyler Wu Collaborative

Oyler Wu Collaborative is a Los Angeles-based architecture and design firm founded by Dwayne Oyler and Jenny Wu. The firm is recognized for its experimentation in fabrication, material research, and design work that challenges the typical vision of the built environment.

Relocating from New York to Los Angeles in 2004, their office has utilized the last 14 years to establish a way of working that is committed to experimentation through a rigorous hands-on approach. Eager to test new ideas, utilize emerging technologies, and explore their work at a larger scale, the office transformed projects with modest budgets into relevant contemporary architectural projects. The work has been driven by an insistence on striking a balance for design experimentation and technical feasibility, often finding creative solutions in the zones between the two. Their recent works encompass a variety of scales from installations to institutional buildings and large infrastructural projects.

Pop-Up Exhibitions

Since Fall 2017, the second semester of the Pratt Session series, a Pop-Up Exhibition has been associated with each Session; thanks to the suggestion of one of our younger faculty members who has taken on the role of our Special Projects Coordinator. As a graduate program, in an architecture school that is part of a larger art and design institute with vibrant departments of fine art, communications, and industrial design, we thought it would be prudent to use the sessions to engage audiences in those related disciplines and praxes. Their works are reproduced and projected forming a point of interest and extended opportunity for debate and query during our post session receptions; now fully instituted for every session. Pop-Up Exhibitions and artists for Sessions that occurred prior to the commencement of this initiative were retrospectively selected and are included here.

Each participant has nominated an artist whose work they find compelling and related to both the subject at hand (Mediums or Contexts) and their individual work and/or interests. The specific works included in this book (and in the live exhibitions) may have been chosen by the participant, the artist, or us. Each artist and/or their representatives were involved in the process of selection where (to our pleasant surprise and on very short notice) all were receptive, supportive, often engaging us directly and often attending the Sessions.

The curatorial trajectory of such a broad and open-ended initiative has a productive looseness that allows us to expand into and include other disciplines in the sessions. Some of the Session participants incite the artists directly and they are all introduced in David Erdman's introductions, however, their work and the intentions behind its inclusion are often left for students and the audience to draw their own conclusions and make connections.

Whether this might be perceived as the antithesis of curation and/or an experiment in collective curation, it is nonetheless an impressive roster of artists and an indubitable collection of stunning work. With a range of more or less established artists whose praxes oscillate from visual arts, industrial design, land art, culinary art, and just dead on intermedia the content on the following pages expands (beyond expectation) our understanding of "architectural" contexts and mediums into a broader field of intellectual discourse. Through mediums ranging from photography, colossal textiles, dirt, thick viscous fluids, drawing, and cinema each contribution allows us to draw upon not only the mediums sessions in a more focused manner, but also widens our understanding of each designer or thinker's understanding of the term.

Similarly, the manners by which artists document, replicate, falsify, mirror, or reflect contexts, be it of a gallery, courtyard, or landscape, their work enriches and deepens the prospect of new ways to conceive of context. The following pages could perhaps be seen as a visual epilogue, a meditation on the palindromic bookends (Mediums and Contexts), on the center-piece introductions and essays, allowing one to interlace the ideas captured throughout the book and enticing one to project and explore them further.

Images of Pop-Up Exhibitions and Receptions following Pratt Sessions

M

Philipp Schaerer, *Bildbau No 2* (left) and *Bildbau No 5* (right)
2007
(Artist selected by Young & Ayata)

Fiona Connor, *Something Transparent (please go round the back)*
Michael Lett, Auckland 2009
(Artist selected by Sylvia Lavin)

Thomas Demand, *Control Room*
2011
(Artist selected by Elizabeth Diller)

Janet Echelman, *1.8 Renwick, Washington, D.C.*
2015
(Artist selected by Oyler Wu Collaborative)

Acknowledgments

DAVID ERDMAN
CHAIRPERSON, ASSOCIATE PROFESSOR
GRADUATE ARCHITECTURE + URBAN DESIGN

This book would not have been possible without the generous time and support of each participant in the Pratt Sessions. Their willingness to engage in a non-standard, conversation-based format, to make the extra effort to custom build presentations and to open themselves up to unpredictable subjects and discussions are all reconfirmations of their station as leaders and their insatiable curiosity as thinkers. Their counterpart artist nominees for the Pop-Up Exhibitions deserve special thanks as well, for their willingness to share their work in relation to these Sessions with the students and faculty of the GAUD, School of Architecture, and Institute at large. I would like to especially thank dean Tom Hanrahan for his willing support on this project and for extending the latitude to enrich the public programs and printed discourse of the School of Architecture with specific respect to the GAUD. I would like to equally thank Kirk Pillow, provost, whose comprehensive support of this project has enabled us to galvanize our interests and capacities as a department and faculty within the local, national, and international design and arts communities.

Without student interest none of this would be possible and I would like to specifically thank the Graduate Student Council members for their support and participation in these events. I would also like to thank all faculty who have attended these events, asked questions, participated in and/or contributed to this book, not only for their efforts but also for exploring these subjects unfettered and allowing us the collaborative space to test and debate them in an exceptional and rare showing of collegiality and collective will.

Behind the book and each of the events is an impeccable team of colleagues who have been the pillars upon which all of this is possible. Our editor Julia van den Hout and her team at Original Copy, as well as Jeff Anderson, the GAUD Special Projects Coordinator, have been unwavering in their efforts and commitment to this project, finessing all the errors and collaborating to curate and shape the content in the most meaningful ways. We are very thankful for Gordon Goff, Kirby Anderson, and Jake Anderson of ORO for their support and their assistance with this publication. Special thanks go out to the current and former Assistant Chairs (Alex Barker and Phil Parker, respectively) whose input, insights, and collaboration have been invaluable throughout the Sessions. Erin Murphy, Gloria Nyaega, and Geoff Olsen, who run and oversee the operations of the GAUD office and the IT staff, all help in different ways to prepare and manage each event and ensure that all participants are warmly welcomed to the GAUD, and that all goes smoothly. Last but not least, we thank the many student graduate assistants over the past year—Jacob Myers, Haya Alnibari, Yomna Dabat, Jeffrey Gaudet, and Nai Hua Chen have been the engine behind the preparation and research for each these events and this book.

Image Credits, Mediums

6	Florencia Pita and Jackilin Hah Bloom
7	Young & Ayata
8	Florencia Pita and Jackilin Hah Bloom
9	Young & Ayata
12-17	Florencia Pita and Jackilin Hah Bloom
18-23	Young & Ayata
25	Courtesy of Pratt Institute, GAUD
28	Diller Scofidio + Renfro
29	Sylvia Lavin
30	1-2. Diller Scofidio + Renfro / 3. Matthew Johnson / 4. Michael Moran / 5. Elizabeth Daniels / 6. Cesar Rubio / 7. Nic Lehoux / 8. Beat Widmer / 9. Diller Scofidio + Renfro
31	10. The MIT Press / 11. Princeton University Press / 12. The Architectural Association / 13. Chicago Architecture Biennial, Steve Hall / 14-15. Sylvia Lavin / 16-17. CCA, Montréal
34	[top] Matthew Johnson; [bottom] Diller Scofidio + Renfro
35	Brett Beyer
36	Luc Boegly
37	Brett Beyer
38-39	Luc Boegly
40	CCA
41	[top] Eredi Aldo Rossi, courtesy Fondazione Aldo Rossi; [bottom] CCA
42-43	CCA
45	Courtesy of Pratt Institute, GAUD
47	Tina Barney
48	Aranda\Lasch
49	Po Yao Shih
50	1. Alex Terzich / 2-3. Aranda\Lasch / 4. Danielle Venturelli / 5-6. Aranda\Lasch / 7. Lala Pereira / 8-10. Aranda\Lasch
51	Oyler Wu Collaborative
54-55	Aranda\Lasch
56	Robin Hill
57-59	Aranda\Lasch
60-65	Oyler Wu Collaborative
67	Courtesy of Pratt Institute, GAUD
M3-4	Courtesy of Pratt Institute, GAUD
M11	[left] Florencia Pita; [right] Corot Wang
M12	Young & Ayata
M13	Geordie Wood
M14	Richard Shulman
M15	Aranda\Lasch
M16	Oyler Wu Collaborative
M18	Courtesy of Pratt Institute, GAUD
M19	Leslie Wayne. Courtesy of the artist and Jack Shainman Gallery, New York.
M20	Philipp Schaerer
M21	Fiona Connor
M22	Thomas Demand
M23	Casey Reas
M24	Janet Echelman

APPLIED RESEARCH +DESIGN PUBLISHING

Published by Applied Research and Design Publishing, an imprint of ORO Editions.
Gordon Goff: Publisher

www.appliedresearchanddesign.com
info@appliedresearchanddesign.com

Graphic Design: Jeffrey Anderson
Editor: Original Copy
AR+D Project Coordinator: Jake Anderson

10 9 8 7 6 5 4 3 2 1 First Edition

ISBN: 978-1-943532-23-0

Color Separations and Printing: ORO Group Ltd.
Printed in China.

AR+D Publishing makes a continuous effort to minimize the overall carbon footprint of its publications. As part of this goal, AR+D, in association with Global ReLeaf, arranges to plant trees to replace those used in the manufacturing of the paper produced for its books. Global ReLeaf is an international campaign run by American Forests, one of the world's oldest nonprofit conservation organizations. Global ReLeaf is American Forests' education and action program that helps individuals, organizations, agencies, and corporations improve the local and global environment by planting and caring for trees.

Acknowledgments

DAVID ERDMAN
CHAIRPERSON, ASSOCIATE PROFESSOR
GRADUATE ARCHITECTURE + URBAN DESIGN

This book would not have been possible without the generous time and support of each participant in the Pratt Sessions. Their willingness to engage in a non-standard, conversation-based format, to make the extra effort to custom build presentations and to open themselves up to unpredictable subjects and discussions are all reconfirmations of their station as leaders and their insatiable curiosity as thinkers. Their counterpart artist nominees for the Pop-Up Exhibitions deserve special thanks as well, for their willingness to share their work in relation to these Sessions with the students and faculty of the GAUD, School of Architecture, and Institute at large. I would like to especially thank dean Tom Hanrahan for his willing support on this project and for extending the latitude to enrich the public programs and printed discourse of the School of Architecture with specific respect to the GAUD. I would like to equally thank Kirk Pillow, provost, whose comprehensive support of this project has enabled us to galvanize our interests and capacities as a department and faculty within the local, national, and international design and arts communities.

Without student interest none of this would be possible and I would like to specifically thank the Graduate Student Council members for their support and participation in these events. I would also like to thank all faculty who have attended these events, asked questions, participated in and/or contributed to this book, not only for their efforts but also for exploring these subjects unfettered and allowing us the collaborative space to test and debate them in an exceptional and rare showing of collegiality and collective will.

Behind the book and each of the events is an impeccable team of colleagues who have been the pillars upon which all of this is possible. Our editor Julia van den Hout and her team at Original Copy, as well as Jeff Anderson, the GAUD Special Projects Coordinator, have been unwavering in their efforts and commitment to this project, finessing all the errors and collaborating to curate and shape the content in the most meaningful ways. We are very thankful for Gordon Goff, Kirby Anderson, and Jake Anderson of ORO for their support and their assistance with this publication. Special thanks go out to the current and former Assistant Chairs (Alex Barker and Phil Parker, respectively) whose input, insights, and collaboration have been invaluable throughout the Sessions. Erin Murphy, Gloria Nyaega, and Geoff Olsen, who run and oversee the operations of the GAUD office and the IT staff, all help in different ways to prepare and manage each event and insure that all participants are warmly welcomed to the GAUD, and that all goes smoothly. Last but not least, we thank the many student graduate assistants over the past year—Jacob Myers, Haya Alnibari, Yomna Dabat, Jeffrey Gaudet, and Nai Hua Chen have been the engine behind the preparation and research for each these events and this book.

Image Credits, Contexts

Page	Credit
6	Christian Richters
7	Amy Barkom
8	1-2. Christian Richters / 3. Michael Maltzan Architecture, Inc. / 4. Christian Richters / 5. Michael Maltzan Architecture, Inc. / 6-7. Paul Dingman / 8-9. Michael Maltzan Architecture, Inc.
9	10. David Joseph / 11. Tom Harris / 12. Robin Hill / 13. SHoP Architects / 14. Magda Biernat / 15. Jeremy Bitterman / 16. Amy Barkow / 17. Ty Cole / 18. Jeff Goldberg/ESTO
12	Michael Maltzan Architecture, Inc.
13-15	Iwan Baan
17	Michael Maltzan Architecture, Inc.
18	Peter Mauss/ESTO
19	[top] SHoP Architects; [bottom] Ty Cole
20-21	SHoP Architects
22	Hayes Davidson
23	Ty Cole
25	Courtesy of Pratt Institute, GAUD
28	Scott Benedict
29	CCA
30	1. Stan Allen / 2-5. Scott Benedict / 6. Stan Allen / 7-8. Michael Moran / 9-10. Stan Allen / 11. Iwan Baan
31	12. Assemblage / 13. Any Corporation / 14. Monacelli Press / 15. Architectural Association / 16-17. CCA / 18. Chicago Architecture Biennial, Tom Harris / 19. University of Illinois at Chicago / 20. Flat Out
38	Stanley Tigerman, The Art Institute of Chicago / Art Resource, NY
39	Stanley Tigerman, Chicago Architectural Club
40	[bottom] Charles Jencks; [top] Alejandro Zaera Polo
43	Courtesy of Pratt Institute, GAUD
48	1-4. Zone Books
49	6. Pelican / 7-10. Graham Harman / 11. Polity
57	Courtesy of Pratt Institute, GAUD
C3-4	Courtesy of Pratt Institute, GAUD
C11	Ron Eshel
C12	SHoP Architects
C13	Stan Allen
C14	Robert Somol
C15	Manuel DeLanda
C16	Ismail Baydaş
C18	Courtesy of Pratt Institute, GAUD
C19	James Welling
C20	Tom Sachs
C21	David Diao
C22	Gary Schafter
C23	Egon Schiele, Public Domain
C24	Mia Feuer

Egon Schiele, *Umarmung*
1917
(Artist selected by Manuel DeLanda)

Mia Feuer, *Totems of the Anthropocene*
2018
(Artist selected by Graham Harman)

David Diao, *BN: His Triangle Paintings*
2011
(Artist selected by Stan Allen)

Gary Schafter, *Small Buddhist Shell, Surface Paintings*
2013-15
(Artist selected by Robert E. Somol)

James Welling, *Ferris Wheel*
2003
(Artist selected by Michael Maltzan)

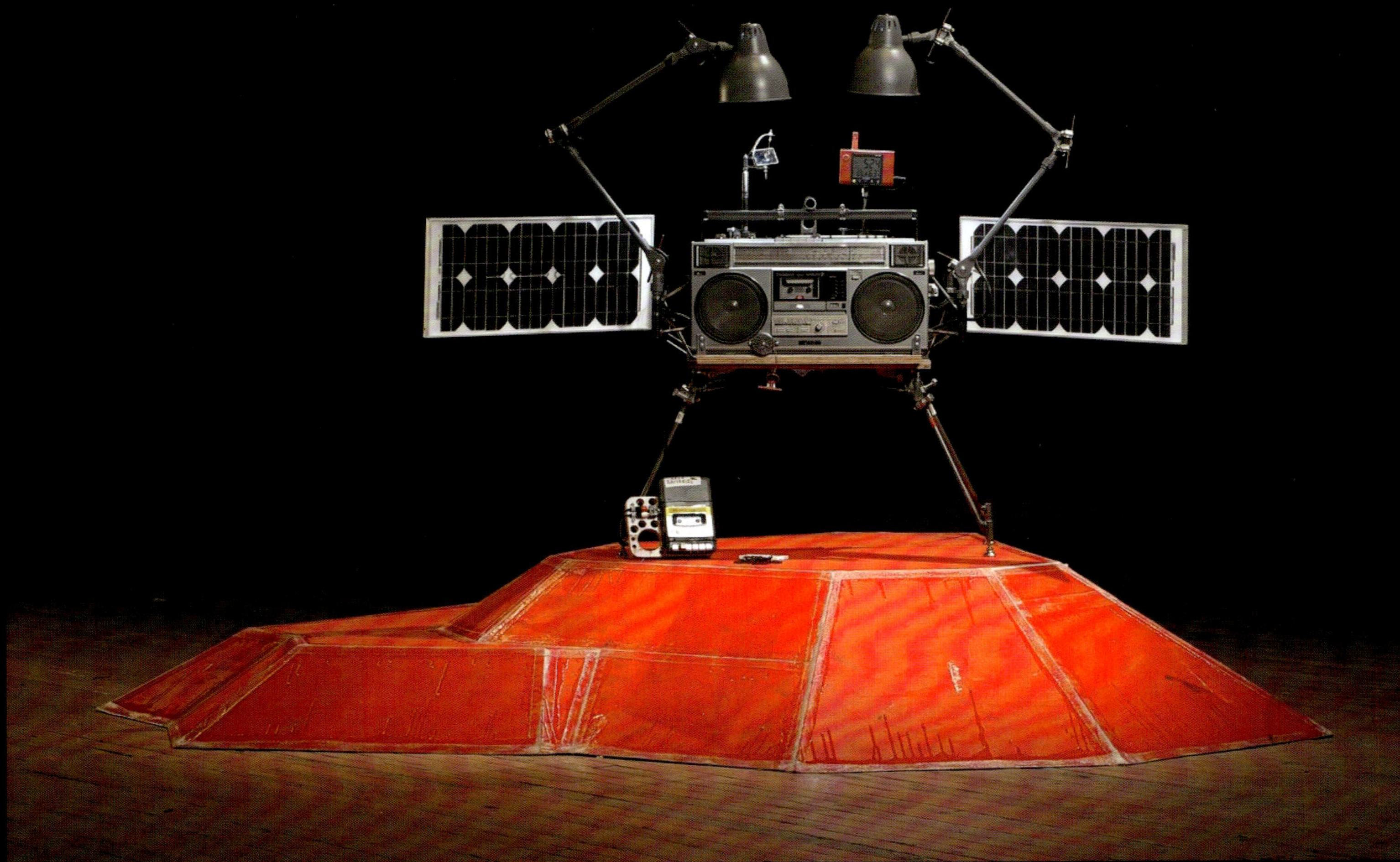

Tom Sachs, *Phonkey*
2011
(Artist selected by Gregg Pasquarelli)

Pop-Up Exhibitions

Since Fall 2017, the second semester of the Pratt Session series, a Pop-Up Exhibition has been associated with each Session; thanks to the suggestion of one of our younger faculty members who has taken on the role of our Special Projects Coordinator. As a graduate program, in an architecture school that is part of a larger art and design institute with vibrant departments of fine art, communications, and industrial design, we thought it would be prudent to use the sessions to engage audiences in those related disciplines and praxes. Their works are reproduced and projected forming a point of interest and extended opportunity for debate and query during our post session receptions; now fully instituted for every session. Pop-Up Exhibitions and artists for Sessions that occurred prior to the commencement of this initiative were retrospectively selected and are included here.

Each participant has nominated an artist whose work they find compelling and related to both the subject at hand (Mediums or Contexts) and their individual work and/or interests. The specific works included in this book (and in the live exhibitions) may have been chosen by the participant, the artist, or us. Each artist and/or their representatives were involved in the process of selection where (to our pleasant surprise and on very short notice) all were receptive, supportive, often engaging us directly and often attending the Sessions.

The curatorial trajectory of such a broad and open-ended initiative has a productive looseness that allows us to expand into and include other disciplines in the sessions. Some of the Session participants incite the artists directly and they are all introduced in David Erdman's introductions, however, their work and the intentions behind its inclusion are often left for students and the audience to draw their own conclusions and make connections.

Whether this might be perceived as the antithesis of curation and/or an experiment in collective curation, it is nonetheless an impressive roster of artists and an indubitable collection of stunning work. With a range of more or less established artists whose praxes oscillate from visual arts, industrial design, land art, culinary art, and just dead on intermedia the content on the following pages expands (beyond expectation) our understanding of "architectural" contexts and mediums into a broader field of intellectual discourse. Through mediums ranging from photography, colossal textiles, dirt, thick viscous fluids, drawing, and cinema each contribution allows us to draw upon not only the mediums sessions in a more focused manner, but also widens our understanding of each designer or thinker's understanding of the term.

Similarly, the manners by which artists document, replicate, falsify, mirror, or reflect contexts, be it of a gallery, courtyard, or landscape, their work enriches and deepens the prospect of new ways to conceive of context. The following pages could perhaps be seen as a visual epilogue, a meditation on the palindromic bookends (Mediums and Contexts), on the center-piece introductions and essays, allowing one to interlace the ideas captured throughout the book and enticing one to project and explore them further.

Images of Pop-Up Exhibitions and Receptions following Pratt Sessions.

Manuel DeLanda is an artist and philosopher. Between 1975 and 1982 he was an independent filmmaker. His films were selected for the Whitney Biennial in 1978 and had one man shows at Anthology Film Archives (1978), Collective for Living Cinema (1980), Millennium (1981). More recently, he has resumed his film-making career, showing his new work at Anthology (2015) and Laboratorio Alameda in Mexico City (2017).

In 1982, he became a computer programmer and independent researcher in cognitive and computer science. Research on the sociology and history of computer science led to the writing of *War in the Age of Intelligent Machines*, published in 1991, on the military origins of computer technology. Since, he has published seven more books, including *A Thousand Years of Nonlinear History* (1997), *Intensive Science and Virtual Philosophy* (2002), *A New Philosophy of Society* (2006), *Deleuze: History and Science* (2010), *Philosophy and Simulation* (2011), and *Philosophical Chemistry* (2015). He currently teaches at the architecture departments of Princeton University, University of Pennsylvania, and Pratt Institute.

Manuel DeLanda

Graham Harman

Graham Harman was born in Iowa City, Iowa on May 9, 1968, the first of three sons born to hippies who met at a Rolling Stones concert in Chicago. He is distinguished professor of Philosophy at the Southern California Institute of Architecture (SCI-Arc) in Los Angeles. From 2000-2016 he taught at the American University in Cairo, leaving at the rank of distinguished university professor. During his years as a doctoral student at DePaul University in Chicago he worked as a sportswriter, an experience he has credited for his readable writing style and prolific output. His authorial debut came in 2002 with *Tool-Being: Heidegger and the Metaphysics of Objects* (Chicago: Open Court). He has continued to publish frequently since then, with his most recent books being *Object-Oriented Ontology: A New Theory of Everything* (London: Pelican, 2018), *Speculative Realism: An Introduction* (Cambridge, UK: Polity, 2018), and *Art and Objects* (Cambridge, UK: Polity, 2019).

He has lectured in 39 countries, and his works have been translated into 21 languages. Harman is also a founding member of two of the most visible philosophical movements of the 21st century: Speculative Realism (launched in London in 2007) and Object-Oriented Ontology (formed in Atlanta in 2010). He is editor-in-chief of the journal *Open Philosophy*, the *Speculative Realism* series editor at Edinburgh University Press, and the *New Metaphysics* series co-editor (with Bruno Latour) at Open Humanities Press. His wife, Necla Demir Harman, is a native of Ankara, Turkey. Together they enjoy world travel, nature, and the seaside.

Stan Allen is an architect working in New York and George Dutton '27 Professor of Architecture at Princeton University. From 2002 to 2012 he was dean of the School of Architecture at Princeton.

His architectural firm SAA/Stan Allen Architect has realized buildings and urban projects in the United States, South America, and Asia. Since 2008 he has received three P/A Awards, five AIA Awards, the John Q. Hejduk Award from Cooper Union, and an Academy Award in Architecture from the American Academy of Arts and Letters. In 2011 Allen was elevated to the AIA College of Fellows and in 2012 he was inducted into the National Academy of Design. In 2016 he was one of 12 architects chosen to represent the United States in the American Pavilion at the XV Venice Biennale, and his work was featured in the 2017 Chicago Biennial "Make New History."

In addition to numerous articles and project reviews, his architectural work is published in *Points + Lines: Diagrams and Projects for the City* and his essays in *Practice: Architecture, Technique and Representation*. The edited collection *Landform Building: Architecture's New Terrain* was published by Lars Müller in 2011. His most recent book, *Four Projects: A Stan Allen Sourcebook*, was published in March 2017 by the Ohio State University and ORO and AR+D Publishers.

Stan Allen

Robert Somol

Robert Somol has been professor and director of the School of Architecture at the University of Illinois at Chicago (UIC) since 2007. He is the editor of *Autonomy and Ideology* and has served on the editorial boards of *Any*, *Log*, and *Flat Out*. His writings have appeared in publications ranging from *Assemblage* to *Wired*, and will appear in his collection of essays, *Nothing to Declare*. For the 2015-16 academic year, Somol was a fellow at UIC's Institute for the Humanities, completing his book manuscript, *This Will Cover That: Writing and Building from the Death of Corbusier to the End of Architecture*, and served as the Baumer Distinguished Visiting Professor at the Ohio State University. He is the co-designer of the award-winning Los Angeles residence "off-use," and developed the installation "Graphic Equalizer" for the 2017 Chicago Architecture Biennial. He is currently working on a fiftieth anniversary publication on architectural education at UIC, entitled *Now + Then: An Occasional History of Architecture @ Chicago*.

Michael Maltzan founded Michael Maltzan Architecture, Inc. in 1995. His projects cross a wide range of typologies, from cultural institutions to city infrastructure. Michael's notable projects include the Moody Center for the Arts at Rice University, MoMA QNS, Star Apartments, the Pittman Dowell Residence, the new Sixth Street Viaduct, MIT Vassar Street Residential Hall, and the Winnipeg Art Gallery Inuit Art Centre. His work has gained international acclaim for innovation in both design and construction and has been widely featured in publications and exhibitions worldwide.

Michael received an M.Arch from the Graduate School of Design, Harvard University, and BFA and B.Arch degrees from the Rhode Island School of Design. Michael is a fellow of the American Institute of Architects, a recipient of the American Academy of Arts and Letters Architecture Award, and the 2016 AIA Los Angeles Gold Medal Honoree.

Michael Maltzan

Gregg Pasquarelli

Since the formation of the studio, SHoP has modeled a new way forward with its unconventional approach to design. At the heart of the firm's method is a willingness to question accepted patterns of practice, coupled with the courage to expand, where necessary, beyond the architect's traditional roles. As a founding principal, Gregg Pasquarelli has been at the center of this collaborative practice for nearly 20 years—leading teams in design, master planning, and real estate development. He has a thorough familiarity working in complex, urban contexts to create dynamic projects that transform their communities. Gregg has served as lead partner on many of the firm's most prominent projects, including the Porter House, the Barclays Center, two miles on the East River Waterfront, 111 West 57th Street, the American Copper Buildings, and Pier 17. His current work includes Fulbright University Vietnam in Ho Chi Minh City, First Avenue's Upper Harbor Terminal Amphitheater in Minneapolis, and Midtown Center, a large mixed-use commercial complex in Washington, D.C. centered around a new public square.

Beyond the studio, Gregg has earned a reputation as a thoughtful leader of his generation of innovative architects and a powerful advocate for design quality and community values in contemporary city-building. Gregg's dedication to moving the profession forward continues in his commitment to lecturing and teaching, where he brings SHoP's message—about the unity of technological invention, artistic inspiration, and public responsibility—to students across the country and around the world. He has lectured and published globally and has held chaired professorships at schools such as Yale University, Columbia University, and the University of Virginia, among others.

SHoP has been recognized with awards such as the Art Basel & Design Miami Design Visionary Award in 2016 and *Fast Company*'s "Most Innovative Architecture Firm in the World" in 2014, and the 2009 National Design Award in Architecture Design, as well as multiple Progressive Architecture and AIA Awards.

Terroir and Truth

SANFORD KWINTER

As the great neurologist Kurt Goldstein taught, "there is simply greater revelation in pathological phenomena." What he was signaling is that the operating system of any organism or ecology would not normally be visible under standard conditions of functioning—its logic would be embedded and largely masked by the explicit, more spectacular display of behaviors and forms.

To gain access to the operations that govern it, to the intelligence that controls the modes of expression, one needs an obstacle, a gap, a resistance, or an interruption of preset routines that causes the system to actively innovate and adapt before one's observing attention. It is through and within these improvisatory performances that deeper understanding becomes possible.

At no time in the history of our own discipline have the motivations behind design work become so cryptic and oblique, like a screen or fog that protects the stylish and growing fecklessness of contemporary pedagogy and practice. Given that so many institutions and practices have not only abandoned the checks-and-balances regimens of "theory" but now often affect explicitly and purposely to renounce it, the wider need for insight and understanding is being pursued by other means. Among these are the growing popularity of the "dyad lecture" in which two related practices and worldviews are brought into relation to generate a differential—no matter small or large—in whose gap the logics of commitment can more clearly be heard and seen. Pratt has commissioned now three year-long sets of such dyadic engagements and it has not shied away from amplifying the discords, controversies, but also the splendors and bankruptcies that such rap battles can implicitly expose.

What has been fascinating is that the revelatory "rifts" do not necessarily, or only, appear within or among the paired presenters (whose generational commonality is almost always preserved), but tellingly between the fulsome consensus the twinned speakers sometimes display and the discrepancy their collective affirmation can generate against a wider historical view or broader awareness of alternative cosmopolitan practice.

What is rich and salvational about such innocent and genuinely collegial dyadic performances is that they generate the function of dissent by their very nature and structure (although sometimes, to be sure, the audience has to call it out) without needing to rely, as in the past, on the courage, principled attitudes, or critical-philosophical labor of the individual actors in question. Pathological revelation is a rich byproduct of these "tender agonisms."

These are then, at their best and most rewarding, forensic practices. But forensics need not only be seen as forms of discovery to elucidate pernicious realities but rather as a methodology for penetrating the veil of gross appearances to achieve greater access to the nuances, admixtures, and creative operations of molecular (meaning underlying, composing) forces, properties, and interactions.

In the world of wine culture, and later across the entire landscape of culinary practice from foraging, farming, mise-en-place, preparation, transformation, expression, presentation, and so on, the concept of "terroir" expresses the infinity of connections that connect what appears on the plate and is delivered to the palate to the specific universe of historical and material conditions in which it was formed. Terroir refers to the infinitely subtle variations of expression that can be extracted

continuously from the earth, climate, culture, and even mindsets present in the ecology that developed and harbored them within the raw products from which they are subsequently refined. In this sense all form and substance is seen as generated by, and inextricably linked to, combinatory relationships that are always specific and timely and subject to capture and elucidation.

The new and cryptic conditions of today's design milieus are ever-more-importantly subject to these same probing operations of exploration, experiment, and interrogation. At no time in recent history have the logical forces that produce design propositions been so obscure in their philosophical foundations or relations to the operations of their own history. Yet every project and practice constitutes the expression of a veiled and mysterious logic or intelligence that may or may not be sound or authentic but which nonetheless represents the full truth or lie of creative formal practice. Every generation of practitioner selects and extracts features and properties from its educational milieu and historical experience and converts these into formal arguments and "facts." To listen and to watch these demonstrations is no different than to open one's sensibilities to the wonders and richesses of material culture as one does at the chef's table or sommelier's cave.

But the question is where and when the cooking and consumption procedures are made to take place, and who takes on the responsibility of concern for the properties of the terroir that lies operational within. Who takes responsibility for the forces that make and shape us? If no longer the architect-at-her/his-table or screen then it must be to those of us who listen, watch, combust, and consume, we who provide the intellectual framework of architectural consumption—who stage and "set up" the pathologies so that they may become more accessible to those who watch than to those who present.

This attitude may be the next necessary phase of architectural—and perhaps all other—education, and it is one that is being increasingly integrated into our pedagogy at Pratt.

Introduction

DAVID ERDMAN
CHAIRPERSON, ASSOCIATE PROFESSOR
GRADUATE ARCHITECTURE + URBAN DESIGN

In surfing, a "session" is a period in which you make something out of nothing. A moment of precision, in which one reads, galvanizes, exploits, and interacts with a consortium of forces. It is as euphoric as it is fleeting, as mysterious as it is understood. Surfers spend their lives craving a good session. The musical equivalent is not so different. Often unpaid, informal gatherings harnessing live performance or improvised recording, one could argue that a good musical session (if witnessed or documented) is the engine behind a musician's growth. Be it musician to musician, human to aquatic medium, or architect to architect, the spirit of the Pratt Sessions is to debate, question and discuss matters on the periphery and core of our discipline. To capture a fleeting moment with some precision and allow it to alter, shift, and transform dynamically.

The Pratt Sessions are conceived as a distributed symposium focused on two parallel research subjects we are currently examining in the Graduate Architecture and Urban Design programs; Architectural Mediums and Contexts. Like a surfing session, these sessions are meant to galvanize something out of subtle aberrations, to read the surface closely, to gain an understanding of its depths, and to have an improvisational one-off quality; each discussion being different and having to negotiate the particularities of that specific event and its participants.

Bringing together pairings of designers and thinkers, one of whom is regional and the other non-regional (predominately from New York City and Los Angeles), the sessions curb stereotypes and assumptions about the thermohaline circulation of architecture discourse; I am here borrowing heavily from surfology, using the term for oceanic swells and current flows as an analogy for the formation of the Kittler-like discourse networks in architecture. The thermohaline circulation of the sessions is an analogy to the redistributing those networks, and their associate cultural/communal bi-products for the GAUD, School of Architecture, Pratt, national and international communities.

Like the oceanographic science of predicting current flows and understanding their engrained patterns, the circuitry of architecture discourse has been in an East to Westward flow in North America since its instantiation in the late 19th and early 20th century, and has been reinscribed and stabilized through the mid- and late 20th century. One could chart this thermohaline flow in higher education as moving from Ivy to Prairie to the Wild Wild West. The intellectual culture of architecture and requisite institutions thus re-inscribe Manifest Destiny often with a pejorative set of associated overtones: the East is where you think about it and the West is where you just do it! Laid back versus uptight, sunny versus cloudy, the climatological and cultural overtones continued to divide East and West Coast cultures and discourse networks until the late 20th century when they began to reverse.

The mechanics of these established modalities of thinking, intellectual culture, and lifestyle are shifting. We feel this acutely here at Pratt—located in a primary cultural hub in Brooklyn. Back flows, ebbs, and reversals of discourse and influence can be seen across the East Coast, even seeping back into Europe where West is now influencing East. Just look at how many teachers, deans, and chairs on the East Coast are former West Coast faculty and vice versa. The curatorial approach of the sessions was to both recognize the established and historical circuitry of discourse while trying to entangle and identify its reversals and ambiguities. The sessions became an immediate and swift way to gauge the degree to which those stereotypes reassert themselves and measure where they fall apart; using the subjects of mediums and contexts as an instigator to fuel the fire.

The participants in the sessions are curated as much for their similarities as they are for their differences. They are asked to focus presentations on the given subject as a means of enriching a precise discourse and to foster student discussion; a central factor in the origins of the series. The discussions have extended for hours after presentations completed and are all followed by continued debate and discussion during the reception and Pop-Up Exhibition, including work from two artists the participants have nominated. The artist inclusions often further enriched the discourse and potential affiliations with subjects and other discourse networks—bearing the fruits of being housed within an art, architecture, and design institute such as Pratt.

My job as the introducer of these events has been not so much to laud my esteemed colleagues nor account for their work in a manner accurate to either their writing or others' writings about their work. Instead it has been to give their work a narrow reading in relation to the theme at hand. I see my introductions, included here with the presentations and conversations, as one part warm up band—priming the arena for the main act—and one part having a productively oblique relationship to what the presenters may or may not show, which was often not known in advance.

This second volume of Pratt Sessions collects six sessions, three focused on each subject, involving seventeen participants; including moderators, spanning one year. Among them are six leading female thinkers and designers, six participants from the west coast and one from the mid-west. While each section is presented chronologically within the two subjects, they are not in the exact order in which they occurred over the course of the year. The subjects and lectures were "interdigitated," allowing for a switching from one subject to the other and to unfold over the semester and year. This configuration produces a rich texture of thinking, a range of opinions, and a productively "selective amnesia" about the subjects at hand. A distinct advantage to distributing a symposium and/or discussion with this type of structure is its capacity for inclusivity, diversity, as well as unanticipated redundancies, overlaps, and bifurcations. The book design is multi-axial in response, using different page orientations—front, back, portrait, and landscape—to coalesce. This was the graphic counterpart to infusing the book with productive yet coarse mixtures of readings with the hope that one might flip between all three sections, and discover this introduction, for example, well after reading other portions of the book. The middle section of this volume collects the proper "front" of the book; now dislocated to the center and in a different page orientation. It gathers introductory material, including an essay by Sanford Kwinter, introduction by former Dean Tom Hanrahan, and the Pop-Up Exhibition artists and artworks. The two sessions sections are mirrored, forming a palindromic structure that allows for reading in two directions. They include edited versions of the introductions I delivered as well as the edited versions of the participants' presentations and the conversations that followed. The book is designed to enable the reader to experience and navigate multiple sessions, browsing and "surfing" between subjects, introductions, and presentations.

This second collection, like the first, owes a great deal to its participants who willingly dove into somewhat unpredictable territory. It is my opinion that it is within this zone of the session that we are the most aware, attentive, and engaged. It is when those flows switch and reverse, open up counterintuitive readings and understandings that one might find a trajectory through the discourse valuable to his or her own work, thinking, or studies.

Dean's Note

TOM HANRAHAN
DEAN OF THE SCHOOL OF ARCHITECTURE

Now in its second year, *Pratt Sessions* is a new publication developed by the Graduate Architecture and Urban Design programs in Pratt Institute's School of Architecture. The school has long been host to a series of innovative publications that not only introduced readers to emerging ideas in architecture and design but presented them in new and experimental forms. Over three decades the *Pratt Journal*, *In Process,* and *TARP* have expanded the boundaries of theoretical, visual, and topical design journals. *Pratt Sessions* joins this distinctive group with its own inventive format, and rich array of completed work and theoretical speculations by some of the most important architects and designers practicing today.

Each section of *Pratt Sessions* is a transcribed public conversation between paired designers and architects, augmented by examples of their work and observations and questions by moderator and chair of Graduate Architecture and Urban Design David Erdman. The results are provocative and unexpected and provide insights into architecture and design that are not always revealed in more traditional lecture formats. Some of these conversations demonstrate broad agreement on critical ideas in design, while others illustrate the unique differences in approach and thinking from this exceptionally talented group of contributors. All of them touch on the most important issues affecting the design of spaces, buildings and cities today. Together they illustrate the remarkable range and complexity of thought that can be found in today's design world.